# Not Child's Play
An Anthology on Brother-Sister Incest

# Not Child's Play

## An Anthology on Brother-Sister Incest

Edited by Risa Shaw

Lunchbox Press, Inc.

Cover design by Mitzi Mize
Cover photo by Sharon Gervasoni
"The Action Girls" photos by Sharon Gervasoni
Book design and production assistance by Megan Klose
Book layout and production consultation by Cissel Gott
Publication services donated by
Communications Development, Washington, DC

Copyright © 2000 by Risa Shaw. Printed in the United States of America. All rights reserved. No portion of this book may be reproduced, distributed or transmitted in any form or by way of any means, including photocopying, recording or other electronic format, without the prior written permission of the publisher. For information contact Lunchbox Press, Inc., Box 5723, Takoma Park, Maryland 20913-0723, or www.LunchboxPress.org.

Publisher's Cataloging-in-Publication Data
Shaw, Risa, 1960 -
Library of Congress Card Catalog Number: 00-192336
ISBN: 0-9704235-0-0
1. Incest. 2. Childhood Sexual abuse. 3. Women. I. Title.

The writings and artwork herein are the sole work of the credited individuals, although some of those bylines may be pseudonyms. Those individuals are solely responsible for the accuracy and truthfulness of their contribution.

This collection is dedicated to all of us
who had so much stolen from us
and to the children
that they may never know such thievery

# Acknowledgments

There is no question that I have the best friends in the world. They came out of the woodwork with unconditional generosity and support as I saw this project to fruition. Their deeds have been countless and their love endless. Encouragement came, always, from friends and from people who simply heard something about this project, many of whom I have yet to meet. To each of you, thank you for your kindness, enthusiasm, wisdom and sweet souls. My deepest gratitude goes to you. Among the many people whose gifts have been both immeasurable and extraordinary, I want to extend my thanks specifically to:

*Riggin Waugh* for her keen editing powers which strengthened this entire book, and for her good humor.

*Megan Klose* for her generous technical expertise, giving of her time and her heart.

*Cinda Van Deursen* for her insider status, information and leads, and her unbending awe at the power of the contents of this book.

*Cissel Gott*, whose enthusiasm is exceeded only by her skill and willingness to help with this project.

*Jeanne Donado* for her way with words, not only encouragement without hesitation, but also her way of honoring this work I was doing, as well as her gentle and clear editing hand. And, her ability to see the light, always.

*Margaret Nash* who knew exactly what I was talking about the first time I spoke of wanting a book, of wanting printed words that I could look at and that could remind me that I was not alone. She helped me know from the beginning that this was possible, and far into its midst that it was real.

*Kathy Keyes* whose words were perfect when I thought there was no way I could see past the overwhelmingness of this project.

*Judith Treesberg* who edited my own writings, and whose eyes and words let me know that she saw that I could do this if I wanted to.

*The women* who created inspired Action Girl Figures as a mirror of their own strength and sense of justice in this world.

*Cynthia Cooke* who saw The Girls leading the way.

*Kathleen Long* and *Chris Elfring*, proofreaders extraordinaire.

*Valerie Warshaw* who jumped right in and went through every word in this text with me.

*The ones* whose generous gifts of money created time and space for me in countless ways.

*Beth Wheeler* whose love and respect I hold dear.

*Anne Dykers* for her gentleness and willingness to sit back with me and look.

*Beck Young* who has been inspiration and friend for as long as I can remember.

*Jeannie Witkin, Lucy Tatman, Karen Malcolm, Cece Lammers, Jennifer Shaw* and *Susan Dery* for their constant sustenance and unrestrained cheer leading.

*Sarah Rauber* for her creative and phenomenally optimistic abilities, and her willingness to be there every step, even when me or one of the Action Girls fell.

*Lynn Bonde* for helping me in such gracious ways to retrieve the gifts that I had hidden so they would not be stolen, and to uncover and ditch the constricting ways I had become so accustomed to living that they seemed to still have a purpose.

*Sharon Gervasoni* who has been there throughout, often quietly, and has contributed more to this conclusion than she will know. And, for her intimate knowledge of what this means to me and to our lives. All my love.

And to *every woman* who sent me a part of themselves, who opened up and even considered contributing to this book... thank you for your gifts to me and to the world which we are changing.

# Contents

**Foreword** 1
One Voice at a Time
*Margaret Randall*

**Introduction** 7
*Risa Shaw*

**Section One: Breaking Spirits**

In My Brother's Care 17
*Amy Blake*

Maybe He Leaves Before Breakfast 19
*Janit*

The Lesson 20
*Patti Tana*

When I Was Four 21
*C. Gordon*

A Typical Childhood Evening 23
*Diane McMahon*

My Monster 24
*Judy Stein*

Memories 25
*Christine Anne Pratt*

Brotherly Love 33
*Tzarina T. Prater*

Night Feeding 35
*Catherine Swanson*

Excerpts from "People, Places, and Parks" 37
*Jeanne Savage*

Voice of Silence 41
*Paula Agranat Hurwitz*

Driver's Ed 42
*Lynne Phoenix*

Playing Dolls 43
*Sarah Elizabeth Barrett*

| | |
|---|---|
| Diary Entry<br>*Michelle* | 47 |
| Preface<br>*Mary Diane Hausman* | 49 |
| That Stuff<br>*Mary Diane Hausman* | 50 |
| Discoveries<br>*Mary Diane Hausman* | 54 |
| Morning<br>*Nancy* | 57 |
| O Brother, Dear Brother Of Mine<br>*M. Omura* | 59 |

**Section Two: Wounded Hearts**

| | |
|---|---|
| How Long Shall I Harbor Sorrow?<br>*Ann Russek* | 63 |
| Memory<br>*C. Gordon* | 64 |
| Soon<br>*C.S.* | 65 |
| Drinking Alone<br>*Ruth Trevarrow* | 66 |
| Doors<br>*Frances Louis* | 67 |
| Daughter<br>*Nancy* | 72 |
| Graveyard<br>*Christine Anne Pratt* | 74 |
| Enough Said<br>*Carolyn* | 75 |
| #56 Ashamed<br>*C.B. Clinton* | 78 |
| #15 Boxed<br>*C.B. Clinton* | 79 |

| | |
|---|---|
| The Therapist's Hope<br>*Catherine Swanson* | 80 |
| Breath<br>*Susan Fredericks* | 81 |
| Dirty Words<br>*NíAódagaín* | 83 |
| Little Blue-Eyed, Dark-Haired Italian Girl<br>*Nancy Lee* | 85 |
| Why I Wake in the East While You Sleep in the West<br>*Jennifer Corse Simon* | 86 |

**Section Three: Shattering Silences**

| | |
|---|---|
| Untitled<br>*C.B. Crowe* | 91 |
| The Sleeping Woman<br>*Christine Anne Pratt* | 92 |
| Out of the Muck<br>*Judy Stein* | 93 |
| The Action Girls<br>*Risa Shaw* | 94 |
| Creating Bugle<br>*Tessa Katz* | 95 |
| Scream<br>*Michelle* | 96 |
| Fragmented<br>*Michelle* | 97 |
| Speak Clearly<br>*Michelle* | 98 |
| Footsteps on the Stairs<br>*Risa Shaw* | 99 |
| anger provoked<br>*Meikil Berry* | 103 |
| Confrontations<br>*Tanya Garig* | 106 |

| | |
|---|---:|
| My Brother<br>*Blanche Woodbury* | 108 |
| The Summons<br>*Kathleen Fleming* | 111 |
| Preface<br>*Judy Stein* | 122 |
| What Do You Tell Your Daughter? A Letter to My Brother<br>*Judy Stein* | 124 |
| Letter to the State Judicial System<br>*Judy Stein* | 126 |
| Preface<br>*Patten O'Brien* | 128 |
| Writing a Wrong: Confrontation By Letter<br>*Patten O'Brien* | 129 |
| After "Sorry"<br>*Amy Blake* | 132 |
| Women Shipyard Workers<br>*Ruth Trevarrow* | 134 |
| **Contributor Notes** | 135 |
| **Resources** | 142 |

# Foreword

# One Voice at a Time
Margaret Randall

Public discourse about incest is a late twentieth century phenomenon, voices made possible by feminism, feminist therapy, and the consequent taking back of women's lives. It has created a literature situated in the long and powerful tradition of women telling our lives, so that our sisters and daughters may have access to theirs. Earliest known examples come to us through the lines of ancient poetry fragments. Then there were songs (the women troubadours come to mind, their voices so different from their male counterparts). Still later we have diaries and recipes and journals. And finally there are today's extraordinary women writers, their novels, scholarly texts, audacious journalism, poetry collections, theater and memoir.

In editing *Not Child's Play*, Risa Shaw makes an invaluable contribution to this historic literature. For a decade or more we have heard from the women, in various stages of recovery, who were abused by fathers, uncles, grandfathers, mothers, or the family friend they were taught to call "uncle." We have also begun to hear from abused men (the patriarchal distortion of power affects them too). We have embraced these courageous stories, and many of us have seen ourselves reflected in the mirrors they hold up. Like all truly passionate literary movements, this one has also begun to suffer its negative counterpart: tracts that pretend to cancel out or delegitimize our memory's truth. The "False Memory

Syndrome" writers represent the defensive echo of a patriarchy threatened by our defiance. We may take their blustering as proof of our own righteous power.

In the rich chorus of voices, until now, we have had little (certainly not a full collection) from women who were sexually abused by their brothers. Perhaps brother-sister abuse has seemed an arena less easily defined. The abusive brother may be only a few years older than the abused sister. Issues of domination and control may be less clear. "Child's play" is too often the term used to label and dismiss this activity when it comes into view (thus the affirmation of the book's title). But, as Shaw makes clear in her introduction, "Brother-sister incest is not about a brother 'experimenting' with sex and the sister he has chosen for that 'experiment.' It is about power and control." As indeed is all abuse, and patriarchy itself.

Brother-sister incest is not about sex. It is not about pleasure. It is about power, pure and simple. As such, it has a great deal in common with one race's enslavement of another, adult abuse of dependent children, a boss's exploitation of those who work for him, a superpower's domination of the developing nations within its sphere of influence.

Incest, however, has a particularity all these other infamies lack. In incest, the victim is preyed upon by the very person or persons whose mandate is to provide unquestioned love and support. In this way, incest is the primal betrayal. When the first of all trusts is broken, it becomes painfully difficult—sometimes impossible—to trust again.

In our society, we have the annoying habit of judging degrees of horror. Perhaps this comes from our socially conditioned penchant for competition. For example, the idea that one type of abuse may be "worse" than another: that being incested by a father may be more hurtful than being incested by a grandfather (the presumption being that the closer the relationship, the deeper the betrayal); that being incested by a mother may be worse than

# Foreword

being incested by a father (because it seems to fly in the face of patriarchal patterns); that battery in a lesbian relationship may be more painful than in one that is heterosexual (again, because the behavior defies accepted order of things). I have listened to a woman offer the self-effacing disclaimer: "Well, my abuse only lasted a few months. Nothing like yours that lasted years." Or another, suffering from melanoma, exclaim "At least I don't have breast cancer." This has too frequently become a way of denying or minimizing her own confusion and fear. None of this is at all useful. Abuse is abuse.

Each of us suffers it in our own particular way, with a multiplicity of factors contributing to the damage done. Each bears our own scars. Each eventually emerges through our own excruciatingly hard work (or doesn't), and each—even assuming recovery—has lost something irretrievable.

Different incest relationships do, however, have different characteristics. Reading the prose and poetry, and viewing the artwork in this book, I was struck by the unique nature of brother-sister incest. Which is not to say it is less horrendous than other incest relationships. Or that it is worse. Only that it is itself, and as such cries out to be recognized.

Let us consider the following. Siblings are almost always of the same generation. While we may acquire and repeat some of our parents' attitudes (often without wishing to), we want to be able to look to our brothers and sisters with special feelings of camaraderie. There is the conscious desire to emulate. Younger siblings naturally look up to those who precede us in years, expecting them to be examples upon whom we may model our own behavior. Because of the patriarchal nature of our society, younger sisters tend to look to older brothers for guidance and protection. When that older brother-younger sister trust is violated, it can be as confusing as it is treacherous.

To be incested by one's brother is a multi-fanged abuse. First there is the social desire to belong—to be "one of the gang," accepted by one's peers. Brother-sister incest destroys this possibility. Then there are one's parents: do they know? Do they condone our agony? Do they excuse or forgive the aggressor, and indicate—either directly or by their failure to act—that what is being perpetrated against us is our fault? A girl child who endures ongoing sexual abuse from a brother suffers patriarchy on a variety of different levels. Hers is a particularly complex dilemma.

Risa Shaw has organized this anthology in an interesting and useful way. Divided into three general sections, her chorus of rebellious voices take us on an all-too-familiar journey. In Section I, the secret festers, taunting every area of the victim's life. In Section II, the secret threatens to tear our life apart, and we seek the help we need to be able to confront it. And in Section III, the secret is told: screamed, whispered, shouted, moaned, sung a cappella into the void. And behold: in the telling we do not die. Rather, we understand we are not alone. And we join the growing number of survivors reclaiming what was taken from us. Some contributors have added a preface or afterword, as well, giving the reader initial fears and/or later follow-up.

"Speaking up and speaking out changes everything," Shaw tells us. And she goes on to share with us the story of one of her contributors who, upon sending in her work, wrote that she was showing her writing for the first time. Simply sending it to someone was liberating enough, this woman said; publication wasn't necessary.

We who are survivors know how vital this telling is. As long as we keep our abuser's secret, we remain in fact complicit with the abuse. In silence we continue to protect the criminal and perpetuate the patriarchy that has become his home. The moment we speak, everything changes. We are on the way to recovering voice, which is the first stage of wholeness.

Women's incest literature has, however, added another dimension to the speaking out. No longer are we content to simply share our stories with sympathetic listeners, speak in recovery groups, or

# Foreword

bear witness in forums of different types. Now we are transforming our victimization into art, the most powerful way to move from sufferer to survivor. If suffering produces art, it transcends itself. Thus, we who have suffered incest and other forms of childhood sexual abuse, reclaim the horror perpetrated against us and convert it into something evocative and immensely positive. Others read and view our work, and are empowered by its gift.

I believe it is significant that women have been pioneers in this movement to produce art from violence. Not only speaking out, but making poetry, fiction, images, theater, dance and song from our pain is, after all, the ultimate refusal to "shut up," "be quiet," "not tell," or "bear in silence"—those dictums urged upon women throughout time.

In *Not Child's Play*, a great chorus of women tell with their art, in a variety of creative forms. Psychologists, artists, writers, teachers, professors, mothers, a day care worker, a librarian, a software analyst, a nurse, an editor, and a belly dancer, to name but a few. The section of Contributor Notes at the end of the volume is compelling beyond a mere introduction of those included. Here we find lesbians and heterosexual women, white women and women of color, mothers and those who have chosen not to have children, widely published writers and writers for whom their poem or story in this book is a first break with silence. One woman lists the year of her birth as 1995; speaking out has given her life. Another's bio reads like a wonderful plea to meet a sister spirit.

*Not Child's Play* is an exquisite contribution to this great speaking out through art, part of the thunderous breakthrough and self-affirmation that tears away at patriarchy, one voice at a time.

—Albuquerque, Summer 1998.

# Introduction
Risa Shaw

It was the end of 1984 when I chose to talk to my mom, dad, step-mother, oldest and next youngest sisters, and my brother about the incest in our family. Their shock was evident—were they shocked by what I was telling them, or that I was unearthing this family secret?

No one seemed "surprised" by the facts. They said it "explained some things," like how much my brother and I were at each other's throats the summer we went camping in Minnesota and why things seemed to be "different" that year. My older sister, aware of patterns of abuse, wondered if it had happened to either of our younger sisters.

When I first approached my brother—my only brother, my older brother—he asked me not to tell anyone else in the family. Then he told me not to tell anyone else at all. He was very upset, mostly because I had already told our older sister and stepmother. He wanted to know why I had not come to him first. He wanted to know how the incest could "bother me so much" at that point, because the previous year I had visited him and we had had such a good time. Plus I had never mentioned it in all these years. *Why now?*

The answer to his question is what compelled me to create this book: Speaking up and speaking out changes everything.

Once I had acknowledged the incest, in 1979, I wanted to hear from other women—their experiences, their thoughts, their anger. Where were the others, the women whose bodies tightened instantly with recognition, who lived the shame, the grief, and the outrage with me? I knew that I was not alone, yet back then there were few books on childhood sexual abuse and not one seriously dealt with incest by brothers to sisters.

And this silence continues. In the past decade, numerous new books have addressed incest, but for me something has always been missing. Brother-sister incest is sometimes mentioned but only in passing. I wanted to hear the voices of the other women who had to live with the fact that it was their brother, not their father or uncle or grandfather, who was the perpetrator. There is an obvious gap in the literature.

The voices and stories in this book speak to survival of brother-sister incest. They show us that our experiences are not isolated incidents and that we are not to blame. They can help us shed our shame, and they provide powerful examples of transformation.

Extracting ourselves from the monster of shame may be our most necessary and grueling work. For we were the convenient sisters, the likely targets. Even though that is all we were, nothing more and nothing less, in our bones lives the grotesque lie that we were at fault: because it began in the first place, because we could not make it stop, because we had done something wrong or something to allow it to happen. Nothing, and I mean NOTHING, is farther from the truth. But keeping the secret of the abuse makes it seem so far from a lie, we can barely see the warped paradigm in which we live.

This book is written to offer some light and to suggest that we neither have to feel helpless nor do we have to mimic the deceit and manipulation that were imposed upon us. This book is written to remind us that we can build lives that do not depend on the strategies that helped us survive during the abuse. It is written to help put these experiences into perspective. The incest is not a virus that regulates our whole being; it is merely one set of experiences out of many. Although bad and wrong, these experiences

## Introduction

did indeed happen. At the same time, these experiences do not dominate us. We do not need to live with this alone or in secrecy. This is not just about us.

It is my hope that our brothers, fathers, mothers, and other family members will read this book and that they too will see that the denial of the existence of incest only perpetuates it. Our families did not protect us against the incest; often they permitted our brothers' actions to continue without intervention. I want them to do something about it now. I want them to actively work against this happening to anyone else—to speak out about the abuse, to build their own consciousness, and that of others, to the facts about brothers sexually abusing sisters. I want them to admit that "experimenting," when accompanied by secrecy and fear of getting caught, is harmful. I want the brothers to see that they used their power over their sisters in inappropriate and destructive and hurtful ways.

And just as we sisters need these reflections for transformations, so do our brothers. If they could honestly confront our childhoods, they would recognize what they learned there, and perhaps recognize where those lessons shape adult lives and relationships with women and children—girlfriends, wives, sisters, daughters, sons and co-workers. I want people to recognize that brother-sister incest is part of the same tradition of violence against girls and children that is woven into the underside of what is sometimes called "family values." I want to expose clearly one more piece of the abuse that is hushed up and considered part of normal life. I hope that as each piece is exposed, the infrastructure that supports incest will crumble a bit more and will eventually collapse.

This type of abuse is not about a brother "experimenting" with sex and the sister he has chosen for that "experiment." It is about power and control. The brother's show of power is present before the first physical touch, and it remains long after the last, often until we confront what has happened to us verbally and openly.

In many types of violence, the attacker exercises his power with a weapon, such as a gun, a stick, a rope or a hand. In incest, the abuser exercises his power by using the girl's body against herself. A young girl's physiological responses to being touched in certain ways and in certain places are weapons used against her. This is compounded by the constraints placed on girls and women in our society surrounding sexuality and pleasure. The sexually abused girl cannot even come close to appropriate anger and disgust at the abuse because she is so steeped in lessons of shame and disgust at her own body and emerging sexuality. We are robbed of any clarity we might have, and the enormous amount of resulting shame becomes another tool of manipulation.

Some combination of the sexual touching and attention as well as the secrecy, threats, enticement and shame are enough to keep the victimized sister quiet, allowing the brother to continue. He promises her special treats, like time alone with him or being able to enter a room that is usually off-limits. To a child, this promise of special attention can mean everything in the world, although she is unaware of what the rest of the promise holds.

Words play a major part in incest—the threats, the promises, the ultimatums. Because of the threats or the shame and self-blame, the sister cannot tell anyone, she cannot ask for help, she cannot explain what is happening to her. The fact that no one else has offered help, no one has stopped the abuse, and no one talked about the incest— especially those people who are supposed to watch out for her—is often internally translated as a warning to say nothing.

We live in a world, in communities, and in families that often ignore issues of power and control over others or that operate with power and control as primary values. What happens when parents fail to protect their children? When they fail to make their homes and bedrooms safe? When they fail to notice when the daughter's behavior changes? What happens when parents fail to take action when they are asked for help in the only ways children know how to ask?

# Introduction

By not noticing or stopping the incest, the parents are failing their daughters. Frequently, the parents say they had no idea or they had a hint that something was not right but couldn't put their finger on it. Thirty years ago, public awareness about incest was nearly nonexistent. Incest cannot be ignored or rationalized. The more we all talk about incest and watch for behaviors that indicate it is occurring, the better chance we have of putting an end to it.

Our society explains away brother-sister incest: "boys will be boys," "you were just kids" or "kids experiment." Many parents dismiss the possibility that such behaviors could happen: "not my kids" and "not in my house." And the brothers say, "what's the big deal, we were just kids" or "nobody got hurt, you went along with it." But didn't they also say, "don't tell anyone," "this is just our little secret," "shhhh," "did anyone see you come up here?" Why did they speak in hushed tones? Why did their eyes dart and watch? Why were they aware of every creak in the house, the barn, or the woods? Why did they offer favors or treats if we promised not to tell? Why did they have to talk us into it and then keep it going when we resisted? Why were they so careful not to get caught?

Brother-sister incest is not child's play, and it is not an accident.

These themes—power, control, threats, secrecy, coercion, attention, sexual acts—appear again and again in the writings and art of the women included in this anthology. These women echo feelings of helplessness, shame, wishing for someone to get them out of this, fear of someone finding out, complicity, physical enjoyment and rationalizing. Like the emotions they explore, much of the work in this collection is raw and personal. This opportunity for women to share their stories has been deeply meaningful. One woman sent me a letter with her prose, telling me I was the first person she had ever shown her writing to and that simply sending it to me was enough; getting published was unimportant.

If answering a stranger's call for contributions can evoke such a profound response, what might reading these stories do for other women? The untold stories would fill volumes on this topic. I often wonder how many other women and girls chose not to send in their own words or images, perhaps for fear that their stories would not "measure up." In this anthology, the artistry is clear—it is often in the stories' rough edges that readers will find the meaning.

Verbal images alone cannot articulate the experiences of many women. For some, the incest happened before they could talk; others cannot or do not want to translate their experience into words. Their physical, psychological or spiritual reality demands nonverbal expression. For readers too, visual images may reach levels for which words are inadequate. The possibilities when color, shapes and use of space interact with the relationships between words and images are endless—and healing. Reflecting on images to describe experiences, feelings and thoughts tap into worlds that are not accessible through words.

Initially, this book was to include as much visual material as written material. I deeply regret that this is not the case. But don't be fooled—art about brother-sister incest abounds. It appears in women's private journals, in sketch pads and on scrap paper. It is featured in art shows. It hangs in people's homes. In 1992 it was the focus of an art show that filled the walls of two galleries and hung in the windows of numerous businesses around our nation's capital. It tells eloquent tales of women breaking their silence and moving through their lives. And in doing so, all of the work about brother-sister incest—whether included in this book or not—invites and entreats viewers to continue speaking out. Each time any one of us speaks up, we help to prevent incest from happening to other girls in the future.

In a sense this book began with those first conversations with my family. For nearly two decades now, I have watched as each of them has responded to his or her own knowledge of the incest in our family. I have watched how I have dealt with the effects of incest on me and the changes that have come with disengaging myself from the control exercised over me.

# Introduction

My younger sister, also a survivor of brother-sister incest, no longer believes that it had no effect on her. As an adult, she saw the damage done by a teenage boy who molested numerous children. That experience changed how she saw her own childhood experience. She and I now talk about the incest. We try to figure out dates and places and other facts that seem to elude us. We talk about responsibility—who carries it now and who carried it back then. We discuss how this abuse occurs because of dynamics in the family as a whole, not just between brother and sister. We wish that our parents—our mother, father and stepmother—had figured out what was going on. Neither of us dwells on the fact that they didn't or that it is possible that our brother was molested when he was younger or that one or more of our parents were molested as well. My sister reminds me of how I used to exercise control over her by "terrorizing" her, and she points out how I mimicked the control dynamics that operated between our brother and each of us. We talk a lot about how hard it is to trust and how easy it is to feel bad about ourselves.

In spite of how easily I am pulled into these bad feelings at times, I also know that time and knowledge do change things. The incest, the anger, the shame, and the feelings of unworthiness and self-hate are no longer looming figures that pull the strings of my everyday life. They are a part of the mix of my memories and experiences, both uncomfortable memories and fond ones. I recall them from time to time, and sometimes I automatically respond from them. But I take control of them—they do not control me.

I continue discovering ways to live differently than I did when the incest was happening. Rarely do I find a need for the coping strategies that drove how I lived for so many years; now they simply get in my way. The incest did leave me with unfathomable feelings of shame and unworthiness. All these experiences are not neatly tucked away in the past, but they no longer explode into my daily life. I now understand a great deal more about the part the

## Risa Shaw

past plays in my life today, and I understand how to move ahead in a life that sustains and nurtures me.

May the voices in this anthology help to sustain and nurture those whose lives have been gripped by incest. Our voices speak. Read us. Think about us. Look for us. Talk to us. Talk about our lives. This is what we have. Our lives. And our stories.

# Section One: Breaking Spirits

Action Girl #5, Star, age 2.

# In My Brother's Care
Amy Blake

Why was I in my brother's room? The reason escapes me. What happened, however, was burned and remains frozen in my body's memory.

"Mom wants me to put YOUR POOL up in the yard. But first there is something I want you to do for me." He was 12, and I looked up to him. He was strong, good looking, and free to do things I could not. My little summer clothes came off easily. Had this happened before? Probably, but how can one know for sure without a memory? Positioned on my back on the bed, the one with the wagon wheel bedspread, I waited. As his tongue and fingers reached my skin, I shivered. When his head disappeared between my legs, I froze. Why would anybody want to do that? I mean that's where you go to the bathroom! Doesn't he know?

Suddenly, I was all alone. There was no feeling with what his tongue did to me. I wish I could have gone to the trees, the sun, up on the ceiling, even into the wagon wheels, but into my head was as far as I could venture. My body lay there empty and lonely, and I remained tucked inside my head, protected against the probing fingers and tongue.

"Do you like it?" he asked as if my answer would matter.

I nodded once, I think, because I thought I had to.

When he finished, he gave me some advice, "Don't tell mom or I'll kill you."

## Amy Blake

I do not remember my parents coming home that evening or what we had for dinner. I am sure though that we tried out my new pool and they never caught on to the payment their son extracted for his labor.

# Maybe He Leaves Before Breakfast

Janit

Scrunched in a fetal position,
I hear the steps creak as he climbs up them.
Half drunk from his adventures in the bar all night,
He comes over to my bed and lies down behind me.

I stiffen, as if being dead could discourage him.
I inhale.
He whispers something against my back,
Satisfies himself.
Frozen with anxiety, I breathe out.
Two younger brothers and a sister lie in the same room.
Certainly they have heard the bed squeak.

Father snores downstairs,
Drowns out any hope
Mother could believe.
Why didn't I yell the first time?
Too late for screaming now.
He leaves.
Wiping the wetness on my sheet, I lock my mouth.

Birds sing outside my window.
The day begins, lonely.
No one talks about Eugene.

*Eugene died of cirrhosis of the liver in February 1984 while I was on holiday in Jamaica. He was 43.*

# The Lesson

Patti Tana

When I reach the school yard,
boys shooting baskets
run toward me
knock me down
spit on me.
A big boy with a cap
pees on me.

Our brothers teach us
we are spittoons
toilets
targets.

Just before death
Virginia Woolf writes
*I still shiver with shame*
*at the memory of my half-brother*
*standing me on a ledge*
*exploring my private parts.*

And my own brother—
flashlight in hand—
pulling down my blanket

# When I Was Four
C. Gordon

When I was four and my brother was ten, I said
    I want to marry you

Play with me.  Please please
And I am laid out on the rug.
We are in my room. I am near the dark
leg of my desk. My dollhouse is red and white brick,
towering on the card table.
My arms are strapped to my side with his belt,
my head and shoulders under the white modular chair,
knees and ankles under the blue modular chair.

At bedtime, I pile my stuffed animals on the lefthand side of the bed,
a wall of bear, dog, and giraffe near the door.
I sing row row row,  twinkle twinkle,  I've been working on the
    railroad,
every song I know. I don't want to hear the footsteps coming
down the hallway toward my room and there they are
they're coming, the squeak from his sneakers,
rustle of jeans, the handle turns, a shaft of hallway light
and there is his hand

## C. Gordon

and either I don't remember what comes next
or I say I don't remember what comes next
or someone said don't remember
what comes are nightmares
I can't sleep on my stomach anymore.

I used to tie up barbie dolls, trap them
under furniture, make them cry out No and then
I would never help them. I left them sobbing under the bed.

# A Typical Childhood Evening

Diane McMahon

Choking as he holds my head down, his cock in my mouth. Pushing, thrusting. It's over. I am sick. I feel dirty.

An evening like all the others.

Max, my stepdad, sneaks up the stairs. "Son, are you in your own room?"

Paul slinks into his room, which is adjacent to mine. "Yes, dad."

Max goes downstairs. My brother is back. I am in the tub. He is peeing all over me, touching me. STOP. Stimulated, he feels my moisture and stiffens. Rams inside me. STOP. Feels good. Lying like a board. Want to move. Afraid it will show feeling. Hate it. Like it. Want to die.

Shame, guilt, feeling good. STOP! I don't want to do this. It'll be over soon. Stiffen, be quiet, maybe he'll go away. Not until he is through. If only—no hope—trapped.

I feel like I am participating. "Be careful, I don't want to get pregnant."

"It's okay, you won't." He assures as his sperm spews over my stomach.

Why is this going on? Every night I think I'll say no, but he begs, he threatens. He is right, no one would believe me over him.

*I have, after three years of therapy, finally started to take control of my life and decision making. Several years of putting up with my brother's (step) abuse left me feeling totally out of control in all aspects of my life, not just the sexual realm. My intimate relationship is still in limbo as I work through trust issues.*

# My Monster
Judy Stein

This drawing was the product of an exercise from the book *Recovery of Your Inner Child* by Lucia Capacchione. The instructions were to draw a picture of your angry child using your "non-dominant" hand.

# Memories

Christine Anne Pratt

I am three years old. I am flattened against the cold, linoleum floor in the bathroom, lying on my back—this tall, angular brother on top of me. There is the discomfort of something heavy and big on top of me and the confusion of why.

I am five the first time I remember the youngest of my three half-brothers touching me sexually. I am in his room, standing up. Richie crouches down close to me, talking softly all the time. He pulls down my Billy the Kid jeans. They have an elastic waistband. He puts his fingers down inside my panties and touches me down there. He is whispering that this is all right, but I feel anxious and confused. And I feel excited to be getting some attention from my big brother. I can hear my mother downstairs in the kitchen.

I am always told not to ever tell my mother or something bad will happen—I fear I will be punished and I am deathly afraid of her ever finding out.

I am five. I follow my ten-year-old brother Richie* into the sheep hut and up the ladder to a small loft. The rungs are wide apart for my short legs but I manage alright. His buddies are all there. I feel the excitement of being included, of something secret. He asks me to lie down with one boy—a fat boy who has no clothes on under a white sheet. I refuse. I stand naked and alone, my back to a small window through which light streams past me onto the straw and the boys lying in the shadows, my joy at inclusion turning to fear and anxiety.

# Christine Anne Pratt

I am six. My two brothers, Richie and Paul*, have got me in a small bedroom. They tie my arms and legs to the bedposts. They tickle me with feathers. They are laughing. I am naked. I am angry. I can't get loose. I hear myself struggling. I am crying. Am I screaming?

Most of the abuse in the early years, that is from five to eleven, occurred on a dirty mattress in the barn loft. Two brothers, at times, stand near me. Richie and Paul are five and eight years older than me. I am shown little black and white magazines with pictures of naked white people with no eyes—none of which makes any sense to me. I am always stripped naked and lain on top of. They always ejaculate between my legs, against my genitals. One brother, Richie, experiments with French kissing. I hate to be kissed. He tries to make me suck his penis. I don't like that either. Once he tells me he could marry me. Another brother, Paul, experiments to see if he can make me have an orgasm by masturbating me with his fingers. I am around nine or ten. After that, I am made to have an orgasm almost every time I am abused.

I have been sick and still have a fever. I'm wearing a long flannel nightgown and lying in my parents' big bed, three-quarters of the way through *Peter Pan*. Richie comes into the bedroom and tries to molest me. I am furious and I tell him over and over to leave me alone. I want to stay in Peter Pan's world. My brother leaves me alone this time. I am eleven.

Richie often grabs at my crotch when I am downstairs on my way to the dinner table—my parents just a room away.

I am at a neighbor's house. I am alone there upstairs with my brother, Richie, and his friend. My brother shows me a bedroom. He wants me to go in there with his friend, but I refuse.

I am playing with a seventh-grade schoolmate near her house. She tells me about her sexual play with another classmate, a boy. I tell her a little about my brothers. She suggests that I could do something with her friend. I put the suggestion out of my mind. Somehow, there's something more real at the thought of doing this outside the family. A secret isn't as real, and I don't want it to be real.

When I am twelve, I get a small leather-bound diary with a brass lock and key for Christmas. It is my first journal. I edit out in my mind the fact that Richie molests me the day in January when I record my first entry. The short passage reveals only that I went skating at the cranberry bog in the afternoon.

I am twelve. Sometimes Richie molests me in the woods and fields near the house because my mother is at home. Once, after a blizzard, we are out of groceries. Richie offers to hike the three miles to the nearest store. I beg to go, too, because I like adventure and doing things the older ones do. And it sounds like fun. Halfway to the store, we pass a state forest. My brother gets me to follow him on a detour. He makes me lie down in the snow so he can masturbate on top of me.

Richie is out in the fields with my younger brother and me. He talks my younger brother into going in another direction while he takes me into the woods. He tries kissing my flat breasts this time. He wants to know if I like it. He likes to suck my genitals.

I am twelve. My mother is really angry, and I'm really scared. She calls us all into the living room. We sit on the sofa—me, my little brother, and Richie. She shows us a pad of paper—a drawing of a man with a big penis. "Fuck me please" is written on the picture.

"Who did this?" she yells, staring at the three of us lined up before her.

"Was it you?" she shouts, waving the pad in front of each of our faces.

"No, no." I can hardly breathe. Finally, I suggest that maybe it was one of the neighbor boys. She lets us go. I run upstairs to the bathroom, to breathe, to cry. My brother comes in soon after. He is angry and says, "It was you, wasn't it?"

"No, no." I shake my head and focus on something, anything outside the window.

## Christine Anne Pratt

My second older brother Paul, a college student eight years older than me, coaxes me into a cottage on our property. He takes something out of his pocket—a rubbery thing that he puts over his penis like a glove. I lie on my back on the top bunk, and my brother rubs my clitoris with his fingers. Then he is about to masturbate between my legs but is interrupted by the sound of my mother's voice calling our names from somewhere outside. I am terrified of being found like this. This is the last time this brother molests me.

I am thirteen. Richie tries to talk me into going upstairs. I know what he wants and I don't want to go. He picks me up and carries me over his shoulder up the backstairs to his bedroom. He tells me to undress and lie down on his bed. I have been conditioned to do this from an early age, so I comply. Then he goes into the bathroom for a few minutes. While he's there, I have a stray thought of escaping, but I'm afraid he'd catch me, so I stay still. He comes back with a clean towel, which he positions under my body. If I move at all, he tells me to lie still. He holds my arms behind me or over my head because sometimes I try to push him away. We have developed a game. He knocks me on the head hard with his fist, and I pretend to go unconscious. He spits on his hand and wipes the spit on my genitals and legs. He tells me to do things like put my hands on his bottom or close my legs or open my legs. He goes up and down, up and down until he ejaculates. Then he mops up the semen between my legs with the towel. He leaves and I am free to go. I dress hurriedly and take a shower. I can't take enough showers.

Once, when I am older—maybe thirteen or fourteen—Richie does it in an outdoor play fort. He tells me to kneel down. He gets behind me and penetrates me for the first and last time. I don't know how I feel about that. All I remember is that it happens and how messy it is later when I go back to the house and semen and urine keep coming out of my rear end into the toilet.

Richie is masturbating on top of me, as usual, this time in Paul's room. The bedsprings are the only things making any noise. He rarely talks to me when he does this, and I never say anything. I'm not breathing; I'm holding everything in. I lie still and stiff as a board. My mother comes home early. I can hear her footsteps down below. I am so scared. My brother doesn't stop; he's going faster and faster. There's nothing I can do.

I am fourteen. It is evening. An argument erupts between my mother and alcoholic father, my brothers' step-father. I don't know what it is about—it's usually about his drinking. I feel scared inside. I am in the living room with my younger brother. Their voices are angry. My father blurts out, "You don't know what your son is doing to Crissie in the barn!" I don't hear his words exactly, but I freeze up as soon as he says this much. My mother yells at Richie, who is nearby. "Is this true?"

He yells back, "NO! He's just drunk—don't listen to him."

No one asks me. But if they did, I would say "no" like the time she held up the drawing of the man with the big penis. I am frozen to my seat, and I feel like the whole world is about to collapse on top of me. As soon as I get a chance, I escape upstairs to the bathroom where I can cry and knock my head against something solid.

I am sixteen now. My twenty-one-year-old brother, Richie, and I go skating at the cranberry bog with my younger brother. At dusk, he makes me lie down in the snowy embankment. He starts to molest me, but he times it so that my younger brother is skating around the acre of ice and too far away to see what is happening. That will be about five minutes. When my younger brother is closer, Richie stops, withdraws his hands from my pants, and skates around the perimeter of ice. As soon as he gets back and my little brother starts off, he is at me again. About the third time of this, he unzips his jeans and masturbates between my legs. He finishes before my little brother gets within range. I am angry as I walk the mile home with my pants sticky and wet with semen.

The next morning, I awaken in my bed around five-thirty. My brother is already on top of me trying to get under the covers. I think it is the first time I have ever been molested in my own room. My room has always been a safe place. I don't want him there and I tell him to leave me alone and go away. I am still half asleep. He forces himself on me and puts my pillow over my face with one hand to keep me quiet. He pulls my nightgown up to my waist and pushes his penis against my vagina. I panic. I am sure I'll get pregnant if he penetrates me. But more than that, I need to protect the one thing they haven't yet violated. I squirm. My struggle awakens my little brother in the next room, and he tries to open the door, which has a broken latch. My big brother can't rape me because he has one hand on the pillow covering my face and the other holding the door shut. He masturbates with his penis against my vagina and between my legs. Then he disappears out my bedroom window.

A few hours later my brother tells me he isn't going to "do it" anymore because, he says, "You don't act natural." It is twelve noon. He tells me this by the porch door just before leaving on an errand with my mother. I hope it is true. I watch him grow smaller as he walks away from the house and disappears into the blue car with my mother. I look out in a daze at the empty driveway. It is a gray March morning. I had my sixteenth birthday a few days ago, and now it feels like something important just happened. All of a sudden, everything outside of me feels very still and quiet. I realize that I can't remember a time when I wasn't being abused.

*I have used pseudonyms for my brothers' names.*

# Memories

*When I approached this project, I first reviewed the drawings and poetry I had produced over several years time, but nothing addressed the incest directly. Every time I sat down to write something new, a profound sadness came over me—a mixture of fear, grief and abhorrence. This went on for several months. Emotionally, I was living in that haunting image of the five year old standing naked in the sheep hut loft, her back to the light of the one small window. I felt dazed and entrapped. All I had left were the memories I had carried with me from my childhood.*

*One day, as I sat facing a blank sheet of paper again, I just pushed these memories out, one by one, unedited and unadorned. In the harsh light of truth, the child I'd abandoned so many years ago began to speak. In her scared-to-the-bone fashion, she documented for the first time what she could never put down in her diary. This is not the free child my parents knew—a joyful, bright, sensitive, imaginative being in love with the world and everyone in it. This is my scared, sexually-abused child, full of shame, who believes she is worthless and unlovable because that is how she feels. This latter child is the one who gradually took over my life by trying to stay hidden and voiceless. She says to me, "I am too sad to make anything beautiful out of this."*

*Incest does this. It takes what was once a joyful, loving being full of potential and pricks her into a deep sleep. It uproots her before she is old enough to put down roots. And it affects every aspect of her life—her sexual development, health, career, relationships and spirituality. My brothers abandoned and betrayed me. My parents, though unintentional, did the same. Then I abandoned me. And that's where the healing can begin. How would my life be different if I could find a way to give that hidden child a place of honor, a hero's welcome, a central role in my life that would be life-affirming rather than life-denying?*

*I applaud all the women who participated in this project and my heart goes out to all the women, men and children who are suffering from child sexual abuse and its aftereffects. I know how hard it is. As*

# Christine Anne Pratt

*I wrote in a letter to one of my brothers recently, "I cannot begin to describe to you how much I have suffered as a result of your behavior and the behavior of your siblings." Fifteen years ago, I confronted all three of my older brothers but got very little response. I confronted Paul again in 1998 and I am now on speaking terms with him. When he met with my therapist and me, I found out that the incest began when I was three years old. Besides my brothers, some neighborhood boys were involved as well. I have recounted one memory with the neighbor boys in this book, but Paul has another, earlier memory involving neighbors.*

*Most of my life I assumed my oldest brother was involved as well but I had no clear memories, nor has Paul. My oldest brother, who I confronted in 2000, has no memory of this either and is genuinely shocked. I started confronting Richie again in 2000 as well, but he has been consistently unable see the incest for what it was or to take any responsibility. I also have a fourth, younger brother who broke contact with the family years ago.*

*My parents are divorced. In confronting my father, it became apparent that he did remember knowing something was going on sexually at a later time but he didn't see the gravity in it nor was he capable of making any intervention.*

*My mother has known about it since I was nineteen and failing in college. It took her another twenty-five years before she asked me what really happened. In 2000, with the help of Paul, I was finally able to motivate her to start talking to her sons. So far, she has talked about the incest with Paul. She is eighty-five years old.*

# Brotherly Love

Tzarina T. Prater

Clouds bothered you
was their gray cast
what you needed
to see the jaundice of my sin
Did it show
the muted black brown
of the yellow
bastard child's eyes

You taught me to draw
no long beige fingers
bleed on white pages
I need to see the grave
of my greatest failure
before my eyes
grow blue with age

I'm tired
of red eyes
tired of your face
when I fuck the victims
of our anger
You were my first piano lesson

## Tzarina T. Prater

Brotherly love
in the palm of my hand
you coaxed
suck it like a lollipop
you want to know
what it is
taking you in my mouth
I gave you pleasure
betrayal by masturbation
I couldn't understand

Your hands
make tattered skies
stained with the blood
of my virginity
You were my first love
but
you will be resurrected
Little chiquita
you called me
your favorite color

yellow

# Night Feeding

Catherine Swanson

In a dark room
where thin white curtains
bend and dance
in the evening breeze,
two beds stand side by side,
but only one child sleeps
under the eaves.
Beyond long windows
that face a pine-shrouded lake
the moon casts an arm of light
across tiny waves
softly touching against
a stone dock.
Alone in the house she sleeps.
The revelry at Auntie's next door
does not disturb
the rise and fall
of her small, flat chest.
Nor the cry of a lonesome loon
calling for his foraging mate.
Nor a fisherman in search of a catch
trolling his motor
past the stone dock.

# Catherine Swanson

Only the squeak
of the screen door below
and the sound
of heavy footsteps
on the stairs
open her eyes.
Awake now, she waits
to suckle the stick
thrust into her mouth,
and sip the sour semen
from its tip.

# Excerpts from "People, Places, and Parks"

Jeanne Savage

Tom and I were assigned the double bed in my parent's room. My parents were having a party downstairs. The other bedrooms were reserved for people I can't remember. My parents probably thought it was better than putting me with Sean. Sean was a year and a half older than me, and we fought a lot. Tom was four years older.

It was a hot night, and we had only a sheet over us. The hall light shone dimly through the cracked open door. Tom had pulled his pajama pants down, then closed his eyes as if he were asleep. He fixed the sheet so that I could take a peek by moving it ever so slightly. I pulled up the sheet. I saw the big long thing. It was like my father's, which I had seen when he was returning to my mother from the bathroom one night. The hallway light was on that night, too.

I could hear them laughing downstairs, but it was quiet in the room. There weren't even breathing sounds, just the whisper of the sheet as I lifted it up. *I was the one* who pulled the sheet up and peeked. That made it *my* fault. I was the one who did all the looking in the dim light of the hallway.

\* \* \* \* \*

I went home after school. No one else was home but my brother Tom. He was reading in the living room. I thought for a moment about how he devoured everything in print, finishing a paperback in hours.

It's hard for me to read, I thought, and threw my school books aside, then climbed the stairs. After I closed the door to the bathroom, Tom quietly slipped upstairs into his room. When I went to my room to change clothes, he appeared in the doorway. He leered at my half-clothed frame and leaned just a little closer. He was, though wiry, strong from all the hockey and football rag-tag activities. He was much taller. He touched both sides of the door frame, filling the space fully. He was bare chested. He spoke with a man's commanding voice. He spoke as if he had a right to everything he wanted. He knew our parents would not be there until supper time. Knew our brother Sean would not be home to get in the way.

"Get in the bed," he ordered. "Come on."

I said nothing. He moved toward my motionless body and touched my waist, then caressed my hips briefly. He patted my bed.

"Here," he said. "I'll take care of everything." Peculiarly, his voice allowed an inflection to sneak in; the slight whine tended to accentuate his sometimes effeminate gestures.

He said nothing while he stripped me of my undershirt and pants. He peered at my frame. The thin line of mouth curled up at the edges, and his brown eyes danced with the highlights of excitement. He shook slightly in anticipation as he opened his pants, then whipped the belt from his waist. He stood in his briefs but did not remove them. Instead, he went quickly to his room and returned with paraphernalia. He dumped another belt and small lengths of rope near the belt he had been wearing.

"Go on, lie down."

I had sat up, staring blankly at the things near my bed.

He almost whispered, "What's the matter, don't you trust me?"

His smile was patronizing as he took my right wrist, encircled it with a belt, then lashed the leather to the bedpost. He placed

## Excerpts from "People, Places, and Parks"

the rest of the riggings at the foot of the bed, then moved to the top left bedpost to secure my other wrist with a belt.

"There. That's not too tight, is it? I wouldn't want to hurt you."

I stared past him, through the windowpane, at Thursday afternoon.

He pulled his briefs down suddenly, exposing a penis with an abundance of black curly little hairs above it and full round testicles beneath. The elastic, being pulled down, caused his genitals to bounce. Having my full attention by now, the organ distracted me while he quickly bound both my ankles to the remaining bedposts. He took a position near the lower end of the bed and peered at my pubic area. I still lacked womanly darkness there. He stroked the inside of my thighs briefly until his fingers nearly touched the labia. His style was to not quite touch there. Just open the legs to look and look. Or lift my buttocks onto a pillow to look.

My frame was as straight and curveless as a young boy's. My body was functionally good for running through fields, swinging on tree limbs, dancing through discovery after discovery. But now, in that bed, in that room, my body was dumbstruck still. He grabbed the base of his shaft and stroked up and down. He put his head down to get a better look. Now I could see only the top of his head, his moist brow, his eyes. He lifted his head several times to make sure he had my attention, to make sure I saw his grin. No daydreaming out the window now. He smacked his lips. I could hear his heavy breathing, then he suddenly sucked in his breath so that I heard no sounds but the slapping sounds as he jerked his organ faster. It would be over soon. He shivered and then his whole body stiffened. I knew the white gooey stuff must be coming out of the tiny hole in the head of his penis.

\* \* \* \* \*

Tom was away in the Navy. I came out of my room and started down the hall toward the stairs. My brother Sean jumped in front of me. He had taken one of my sanitary napkins and thrust it under his exposed genitals.

"N-ya, n-ya," he taunted, "Is this the way you use it?"

"Get away from me."

He laughed and laughed.

* * * * *

Nobody told me. I just knew. Everything was my fault. I was the youngest, but "it" was somehow my fault.

# Voice of Silence

Paula Agranat Hurwitz

I am the voice of silence
Hiding in the closet
Or in a make-believe world.
Why can't they hear my scream?
My whole body resonates
From an inner wail.

I cry out for help
But my voiceless terror
Never reaches their ears.
Each time he nears
A scream leaves the pit of my stomach
But sticks in my throat.

I am the voice of silence
Being carried up the stairs
To play another pain-filled game.
Wherever he touches me
My body cries, Not that.
No more. I love you.

# Driver's Ed

## Lynne Phoenix

Driver's Ed begins in the front seat
with my brother at the wheel
in control
no brakes on my side
no way to stop

One hand grips the wheel
the other grips me
with a promise to let me drive
if I let him
no brakes on my side
no way to stop

He does let me drive
on his lap
the stick is not on the floor
between his legs
I'm too little to reach the brakes
no way to stop

# Playing Dolls

Sarah Elizabeth Barrett

The teddy bear says "no," which is something teddy bears can do. "No. No. No." He says that to all the dolls, even Susie, whose arms are wrapped with adhesive tape so the stuffing won't fall out. She is the mommy doll. There was no daddy doll until the teddy bear came. He arrived when Uncle Carl took Mommy, David, and Joey to the caverns. Mimi went, too. I couldn't go. Mommy said the handrails there are so high that little girls can slip right under them and fall into the caverns. So, Aunt Rose stayed with me and she brought Teddy.

Teddy is a blue and pink bear. Blue is for boys, and pink is for girls. People can buy him before they know if he should be just pink or just blue. Of course, Aunt Rose knew. Maybe the store didn't have just pink bears.

My teddy had a pink ribbon around his neck. One day the ribbon came untied, and Mommy tied it for me. Then it came untied again. It wouldn't stop untying. I didn't know how to tie it. Mimi says little girls should be seen and not heard. So, I took the ribbon off. It wasn't very pretty anyway. I think it's in back of the trunk now, the trunk at the end of my closet.

Sometimes that trunk is just a place to store old quilts. Other times it's a lofty mountain for the dolls to climb. The dolls live in the closet. They live in the space between the clothes, a space just my size. They live there so they won't get

Mimi's house dirty. They have a suitcase, a cradle, and a table with one chair. There were three chairs until David and Joey sat in them. Uncle Carl told them they were too big for my chairs, but they didn't listen. I don't think they had chairs when they were little, so they wanted to sit in mine. They should have listened to Uncle Carl though. They were too big, and the chairs broke. I couldn't fix them, so now I have only one chair.

Susie doesn't sit on the chair. When she is well, she sits on the suitcase under the table. Teddy sits beside her. He cuddles next to her. Susie has a soft cloth body but a very hard head. Where her lips are parted, you can see a little space between her two front teeth. It makes her look like a baby, but she's not a baby. She's the mommy doll. She doesn't smile, and the color has worn off her cheeks. She has adhesive-taped arms and is very old. She is eight, and eight is very old for a doll.

Some days Susie stays in her pajamas all day because she is sick. Then the baby dolls take care of her. She hugs them and tells them what good babies they are.

When Susie is sick, she sleeps in her cradle. I lay her down, and she closes her eyes. She doesn't close them completely though because some of her eyelashes are missing. She's a light sleeper.

Teddy is much bigger than Susie. Maybe he shouldn't be the daddy doll. He might hurt Susie when he lays on top of her. I hold him carefully so all his weight isn't on her. I don't know what else to do. I don't have any other daddy dolls.

Sometimes my brother Joey plays with me. I don't know why he doesn't play with David. One summer, David and Joey's friends played football in our yard every day. I played, too. Then Mommy told me to come inside. I don't know what I did wrong. Maybe she thought I would get hurt. Maybe David and Joey didn't want their little sister bothering them. I don't know. I just know I had to go inside. I couldn't play football anymore. That was the summer David and Joey's friends played in our front yard. I don't know where they play now. Maybe they play in someone else's front yard. Maybe that's where David is.

Mommy and Mimi are downstairs watching TV; I'm in the closet. Joey is watching me from the closet doorway. He wants me to do it with him. I want to play with my dolls. He says if I will do it, I can play with his electric train for half an hour. I don't want to play with his electric train. He says if I will do it, he will play a game of badminton with me; I can start with six points instead of four; I don't want to play badminton. I want to play with my dolls. He says if I will do it, he will build Lego castles with me for thirty minutes. Joey is very fair. He knows you can't ask a favor without giving something in return. I don't want to build Lego castles. Joey won't go away. I say if he will play dolls with me, I will do it. He hates playing dolls. He says he will.

While I undress, I hold my breath so I can hear if anyone climbs the stairs. No one does. They're watching TV. I lay on my bedspread, on my back with my legs spread like Joey showed me. Joey climbs on top of me. He props himself on his elbows so he won't be too heavy for me. Sometimes he puts his thing inside me. He withdraws it so I won't get pregnant even though I'm too young to get pregnant. He just practices. When he withdraws he comes on my stomach. I get sticky. All over my stomach I get sticky. I don't like it. I make faces inside my head so Joey can't see. I don't want to hurt his feelings; it's not his fault; he can't stop it from coming. Today he wants me to touch him; he shows me how to push and pull. I can tell without looking that he is going to come. His thing is getting big and hard. I want it to stop. I try not to squeeze. I want him to stop. I hold my breath. I hate being sticky. But he can't stop. I move away. I still get sticky. I try to hold still; I don't mean to move. I hope Joey didn't see. He hands me some tissue. Then he wipes the bedspread; he misses a spot. I can see it. Why doesn't Mommy?

# Sarah Elizabeth Barrett

When he is through, Joey plays dolls as he promised. He is too big for the closet so we play dolls in the space between Mommy's bed and mine. We sit on the floor. If we sit on Mommy's bed she will be mad. We will wrinkle her fresh sheets and she will be mad. She likes crisp sheets and Joey hates dolls. He doesn't play dolls well. I'd rather play alone. When Mommy comes upstairs to comb her hair, I let Joey go.

# Diary Entry
Michelle

When I chose to deny the truth about my brother and thought I was imagining or making up stories, the truth reappeared in my body like an alien. I was working in the kitchen sautéing mushrooms when I felt a wave of sexual feelings wash over me to the extent that I thought I might climax right there without touch. Beyond the orgasmic feeling, I experienced excruciating pain in my pelvic area and doubled over on the floor. I cried and yelled at my brother as if he were in the room, until I realized I had two small children upstairs and couldn't allow them to see what was happening to me. I found myself demanding in a strong whisper that he leave me alone and get the hell out of my life. Similar experiences happened over and over again. Sometimes I would have a perspective of myself as if I were another person looking from the ceiling or from behind my brother. It felt so confusing because I couldn't figure out who I was until I accepted the notion that I left my body all the time.

Then I had a clearer memory of Chris. I was twelve, which made him fourteen. I was lying in bed, and the creak of the door shot through my body. I stared at the walls and watched the city lights drive across my room. My mind tried to travel beyond the windows, but the cross bars of blinds held me inside. I fixated on the crystal door knob hoping for some magical turn by my mother. I was stuck as the weight of another body invaded my bed. Arms

## Michelle

slid through mine, and then it started gently. A minute later, it felt as if I was pulled apart and pushed down. I thought I was going to break until I was blessed by a spell of numbness. It was as if I were dead and my soul was set free to wander the paths of cracks on the ceiling.

*"Diary Entry" was written in 1993. When I read it two years later, I am struck by the clarity of my writer's voice, which spoke out when I was unable to speak due to shame and self-repression. Today I trust my writer's voice, which brings sound to my voice. This process has created integration, acceptance, and forgiveness.*

# Preface

Mary Diane Hausman

 Though I had clear memories of things that happened to me as a child, it was only when I reached my late thirties that I was finally able to come to terms with those experiences and call them what they were: incest. My writing has been key in my healing process. What I cannot speak, I write. "That Stuff" came out of the very first incest workshop I was involved in; as more memories and information come up, I add to the poem. "Discoveries" is an excerpt from a novel I am writing about growing up in Texas. Writing the book is helping me deal with a multitude of family issues. It has also blown open the secret of incest within my family. When I shared my writings with my younger sister and nieces, they revealed to me that they too had been incested. Up until they read my stories, none of us knew about the others.

# That Stuff

Mary Diane Hausman

I thought I had no right
to claim the pain of
what happened in my family.

What happened for years.
What happens forever
in the silent reels of archived
movies running out of control
in my head.

*You were only kids,*
someone told me once.
*What you did was not that stuff.*
*Don't write about that stuff.*
*Forget about that stuff.*
*It's not like it was your father.*

No. It was not my father.

It was my brother, my sister
it was me.
It was my brother, my sister
it was me.

# That Stuff

We were caught in a
dismembered circle
the five of us,
me in the middle,
the fifth wheel,
the unholy center.

Our circle spread out from
brother to sister
to sister to brother
to sister.
Brother brother
Sister sister.

Then one day Sister married
and Brother-In-Law
Brother-In,
Law of Silence
joined the circle.
But only for me.

He was not a kid.
And me,
I thought I was a kid.
But no, he told me I was a woman.

At eleven
I was a woman?
At twelve?
At thirteen?
At fourteen?

## Mary Diane Hausman

I was a woman for him.
For him,
while Sister lay next to him
on the blanket
in the backyard
under the big night sky
under the quilt.

Sister thought
he wanted only her.
Sister thought
I was just a kid.

Brother-In-Law
brought his friend into
the circle to share me.
To share the little woman.
I didn't know he shared
Little Sister, too.
Little Sister,
smaller than me.

Over the years,
Friend got to go around
the circle
and the circle grew wider.
Sister, me, younger sister,
Daughters.
Big Sister's daughters.
They got to be part of
the circle too.

# That Stuff

We all grew up together.
A family.  A circle.
A dark circle
like the pupil in the
center of Brother-In-Law's
bright eyes.

A dark, frightening circle
None of us knowing
the other's place around
the ring of silence.

Then, something snapped
when I was fifteen.
Snap.
Like a fresh-picked green bean.
Something snapped and
I got out of the circle.

I slid away
no longer desired.
I slid away
on the new blood
of my womanhood.

That's what happened —
I grew up at fifteen.
Not at eleven.
Then I was just a kid.

# Discoveries

Mary Diane Hausman

The first five years of my life seem a succession of bright days running one into the other. Days filled with discoveries laced with Texas heat and the smell of mesquite and cedar from the wooded hills of central Texas.

My discoveries were simple ones, but breathtaking for a five-year-old. Like learning I could see almost the entire emerald body of Lake Travis by climbing to the top of the big live oak tree in our yard. Or that a buzzard can circle endlessly in the heat of day before spiraling down to feed on a dead rattlesnake in the road. I remember discovering that if I floated face down in the lake, my dog Wiggles would swim out and pull me back because she thought I was drowning. A favorite discovery was that the gladiola bulbs I helped Mama plant bloomed into wonderful white, yellow, and red flowers as tall as me.

One day I made a discovery that changed the rest of my life. I found the door to my older brother's room closed. Being a curious kid, I opened it. Doors were rarely closed in our house, and I wondered what my brother Bubba, seven years older than me, was doing.

I opened that door to find my older sister Sissy (four years older than me) lying across Bubba's bed with her pants around her ankles. Bubba stood over her, his pants and underwear crumpled at his feet. When I opened the door, Bubba jumped back, nearly tripping over his jeans.

# Discoveries

"What ya'll doin'?" Even as I asked the question, a little knot began to tighten in my stomach.

Bubba yanked up his jeans, but didn't button them.

"We're playing house, Cassie." His face reddened, and he spoke quickly. He glanced over at Sissy, then back to me. "Wanna play?"

"Okay." As always, I didn't like being left out of anything. But I felt that strange knot in my stomach tighten more.

"Sissy, wait outside." Bubba grabbed Sissy's arm and pulled her off the bed.

Sissy pulled up her panties and pedal pushers. "All right, but hurry up. Cassie, you can't tell nobody, you hear? And if you do, you know what's gonna happen to you." She shoved me toward the bed.

I knew. I had been threatened the whole of my five years by Sissy and Bubba. I had seen Bubba chase after Sissy with scissors or rocks often enough to know his capabilities. And with Sissy in cahoots, well, they might just take me up into the woods and get me lost, and leave me there as they so often said they would.

Sissy closed the door behind her. I walked over to the bed and looked up at Bubba.

He took me by the waist and heaved me up onto the edge of the bed. Then he pulled at the elastic on my shorts.

"Bubba, no." I became afraid, and wrapped my arms around my waist.

"Cassie, you wanna play, you got to do what I say. Now, I'm the daddy, and you be the mama."

He pushed me back on the bed. I looked up at the ceiling and stared hard. My stomach tightened more as I felt Bubba's bare chest, sweaty and bony, press on top of me. I squirmed when he pulled at my legs, and he gripped my left ankle tight. It hurt, but not as much as when he pushed himself inside me. It was the strangest feeling I had ever felt. Pain, mixed up with a tingling. I started to cry.

Bubba said, "Shut up, now. Just be quiet."

He bounced and pushed, breathing hard. I had never heard him make such funny sounds. I kept staring at the ceiling, not daring to look at him. I thought, if I look at him, something very bad will happen. Like maybe the ceiling will fall. Or Mama will come in, although I knew Mama was at a Tupperware party up the hill at the Spring sisters' house. She had taken my baby brother, Rory with her.

I thought I could keep the ceiling up and make everything still and fine just by staring hard and not looking at Bubba.

It hurt having Bubba push himself inside me, but there was also a strange sensation of pleasure. It almost felt like when I touched myself. It *almost* felt good. But I knew, even without Bubba's and Sissy's threats, this adventure was not one to tell about.

Finally, Bubba gasped and pulled his sweaty body off me. I took my eyes off the ceiling and looked at him just as he tucked his red penis into his underwear and pulled his jeans up.

I started to whimper, then to cry. I didn't know why I was crying.

"Cassie, quit bawling! Now, you go out and play and shut up!" Bubba opened the door and left. I heard him run across the living room, up the steps into the bathroom. I didn't know where Sissy had gone. The house was quiet.

I climbed down off the bed and pulled up my own panties and shorts. I wished I had not made this discovery. I went outside and sat on my rocking horse. I was sore between my legs. Rocking on the horse wasn't such a good idea after all. I got off my horse and sat down beside it and cried. I cried until I looked up at the sky and noticed storm clouds gathering. I stood up and walked over to Mama's garden. I stuck sticks in the dirt alongside the gladiola stalks so they wouldn't get beaten down in case it rained.

# Morning
Nancy

The creaking floorboards in the hallway usually alerted me. A flush of fear gripped my heart, then radiated quickly across my body as if to add another protective layer. I had been wearing my robe to bed over my nightgown and then twisting in my sheets to make access to my flesh difficult. Maybe he would give up this time. Maybe he would go away.

My brother turned the corner into my room. I couldn't see him because my eyes were pressed closed, pretending to sleep, but every pore of my skin knew he was there. I heard his shallow, raspy breath. I smelled his greasy, oily, teenaged boy smell. And his musty, sweaty, penis smell. I could go away, escape from everything except those smells.

It was dawn. It was always at the first light, when no one was awake, before the sound of the first alarm clock. The house was especially still, extraordinarily quiet. Whatever awoke him to his post-nocturnal pursuit was not just a genetic stirring. In this case, it was hereditary.

He began the slow, purposeful peeling. First he peeled back the sheets, then he tugged at my robe and gown. Slow, painfully slow, so as not to awaken me. It took even longer now, and I couldn't stand it. When he had exposed enough of me to look at and to touch, he would press his hands on my just developing breasts. He would squeeze his fingers between my legs. He

## Nancy

would fumble with one hand in his own pants. I didn't want him to see my eyes twitch, so I kept my head turned away. With my face stuffed in the pillow, I thought I would suffocate while trying to hide my fear, my disgust, and my shame.

When I couldn't stand it, I would move, like I was a sleeping person getting into a more comfortable sleeping position. If I got angry, I would roll onto my stomach and lie flat so the things he most wanted to touch were not available.

When I moved, he would retreat a few steps, wait a few moments, then press forward again. I held my breath each time, hoping I had scared him away. I knew he was afraid, I could tell by his uneven breathing.

Why didn't I tell my brother to stop? Why didn't I call out for help? What I knew then was too complicated to put into words. I was only ten.

We were both afraid of the same thing—my father. Without words, we both knew that if my father woke up he would beat my brother senseless, and then blame me. Then he would beat me, too.

I knew that my father would blame me because my brother didn't control himself.

I knew my father felt I was his possession and no one else should touch me.

I knew my father blamed me for what he, too, had done, because somehow being female meant men would want to touch you—but it wasn't their fault.

I knew my mother wouldn't protect me. She didn't have a voice. She had turned it in with her wedding vows.

I knew all this by the time I was ten years old. Whatever men did to me was my own fault. I would have to find my own voice—and learn to say no.

# O Brother, Dear Brother Of Mine

M. Omura

They call it bad touch now
For what had no name back then

Dark stairs creaking
Fingertips awakening
The sleeping landscape of my body

Two years of feigning death
Fear and inner terror consume me
At night, I live the dead animal syndrome

I was maybe eleven
I had no words, no screams, no help
Mom, Dad—please, help me to tell you
You should have known better

Your karmic past will continue to haunt you
As you pay with seven past wives
Wanting more, having less
What is your story?

## M. Omura

My son and daughters
Are safe from your ways
Your touch
Armed with words, with screams, with help
Each will tell

Bad touch then
A decaying memory now
But somehow I thank you

For you have given me myself to rely on
Have given me my words to speak out with
Have given me power over my past
And I have given you
Nothing
O brother, dear brother of mine

# Section Two: Wounded Hearts

Action Girl #2, Buzz, age 10.

# How Long Shall I Harbor Sorrow?

Ann Russek

I am not certain
what brings me here
to the Pleasant Mount Methodist Chapel
to watch you, my older brother, marry
for the third time in your barely
thirty years. The ceiling, water damaged,
casts shadows of brown satans
and saints across thin acoustic tile.

I stand beside your only daughter,
reach out to smooth her bright red hair.
It is so obvious she's yours.
And then I know why I've come.

Did you touch her like you once did me,
behind locked bedroom and closed closet doors?
Did your first wife gather her up and leave
without reason, without warning
because she saw a sorrow
settle, too soon, in those not yet knowing eyes?

When you walk down the aisle, your daughter smiles,
your eyes meet hers
and the saints
on the ceiling sing soft blessed hymns with us.

# Memory
## C. Gordon

The baby keeps her eyes
shut. The baby keeps
her eyes open. Her
brother is nine.
He pokes his hands
into her crib. He fingers
her soft spots.
He slides his hand
under her diaper.
It doesn't matter
what she sees.
It doesn't matter that she
can't talk. Her body
stores this for her. Later,
she will remember
when she tries
to put a tampon in,
though she doesn't know
she's remembering.
The memory takes
the form of hate.
She will hate that feeling,
her own skin parting.
She hates what opens in her, that stretch.

# Soon

C.S.

One day, maybe, peeling onions for a winter's chili,
I'll cry.

One day, maybe, standing in line beside a shy dark-eyed child,
I'll cry tears.

One day, maybe, in front of a new birthday mirror,
I'll cry my hot tears.

# Drinking Alone
Litho crayon on paper, 1985

Ruth Trevarrow

This drawing is about isolation. That is what I felt a lot of before getting sober and facing the effects of being sexually abused by my oldest brother.

# Doors

Frances Louis

When I was a teenager, I lived in a bedroom that had no door. Actually, the room was originally equipped with a door, but the door no longer fit properly and would lean against the frame, hanging off its hinges. It was simply too big for its frame—a symbol of the many large things that forced themselves to fit into the framework of my family's life. I no longer fail to recognize this metaphor, although it has taken me nearly fifteen years to have the courage to say so.

Because my bedroom had no door, my older brother was free to come in and out of my bedroom at night without obstacles. He did not need to fumble with a lock or worry about the creak of a hinge. I was fair game. All he needed to do was to tilt the door an inch or so and allow himself in.

There was nothing to stop him.

At first when he came, it was like a dream. I would wake up with my body turned toward the daisy-covered wallpaper that my mother had chosen for me. In the darkness of my bedroom, the daisies seemed huge, their overly bright petals with their yellow centers coming out at me like a threat. There was nothing cheerful about those daisies. The blankets would be pulled down to expose my back and legs, my underwear pulled down around my buttocks, the nightgown pulled high above my waist.

*Caught with my pants down.* I could hear those words reverberating in my brain.

When I turned over to fix my blankets and pull my underwear back up, I would find him standing there in his underwear with my door hanging limp on its frame. He would turn like a flash and be out the door and into the bathroom next to my room, where he would remain for up to an hour. I did not allow myself to think about what he might be doing in there.

I remember thinking that it was the dog who had done this, taken my pants down and stared at me. She would stand by my bed in her innocence, sniffing at my mussed blankets and blinking her deep brown eyes at me. It couldn't have been the dog, I thought. But worse, it couldn't have been my brother.

These visits continued from time to time for most of my thirteenth year. The scenario was always the same — door hanging, flash of recognition, and then the sight of my brother's white underwear as he fled the room. It was always terribly dark, and the dog would stand by my bed, her eyes wide and questioning, as if she too were not sure that what she'd seen was real.

I was not alone in my abuse. My mother, who has taken and shared many of the things I have not always been willing to give her, informed me some time later that my brother had been visiting her at night as well. I remember some of the things she said: "You, too? He's been looking at you?" But for some reason I cannot remember the look on her face when I revealed that he had been coming into my room at night. It must have been shock, anger. Or perhaps relief at no longer being alone in this. My mother, by her own admission, is not the kind of person who can take being alone.

By this time I had abandoned my doorless room for the haven of the living room sofa. Although the living room was also without doors, I somehow felt safer in an open space that all the family shared. Surely he wouldn't invade the entire family's space the way that he had invaded mine. But I was wrong. He continued to disturb me even there in the open living room, even when the lights were on. My father stayed up late and would often read the newspaper in the bathroom; I was sure I'd be safe with Dad so close. But that did not stop my brother. I woke up with a wetness on my lips (that I now assume was kissing because anything else is unthinkable) and his finger up inside my cotton underwear. I remember how I longed to scream, to feel the release of air and sound pulsing from my lungs. Instead I lay on that couch with my heart screaming inside me, the blood pulsing in my ears, while my father flushed the toilet and my brother ran and locked himself in his bedroom.

Yes, his room had a door.

It was on that couch that I awoke one morning to the sounds of my mother's sobs, the unintelligible words that came garbling from the kitchen. He had touched her, she said, with my father right there in bed beside her. He was getting more brazen. Something needed to be done.

Yet the door of my room still hung off its hinges, a reminder of all the things that were unresolved in that house.

Their answer was to have my father confront him. "I'll get you a hooker," he said, "but your mother and sister are off limits." This was my father, with his usual finesse in discussing family matters. My brother cried, and for a very short time there was talk of counseling—for him, never for me. He attended one or two sessions with the school psychologist to discuss his cutting class, not these incidents. This, too, died down soon enough, and we went on with our lives, like so many times before, pretending that nothing was amiss.

"Boys are over stimulated at this age," my mother said. "It's not that unusual."

For a time I was able to sleep in my bedroom again, undisturbed. By then I'd devised a series of barricades that held the door against the frame and would surely fall if he tried to come in. I pressed an old chair against the door, together with a mirror poised up against it and several large books to weigh the chair down. The noise would save me, I thought. Surely the sound of glass breaking and the thud of books hitting the floor would deter him. At the very least, it would wake the others. If they all were awakened, there could no longer be any denial.

He began to come again some time later, and I then moved from my bedroom to the floor next to my parents' bed. I insisted on sleeping beside their bed for protection. I no longer trusted the barricade or any other part of that house. At least with my father there and the dog on the floor beside me, I could give myself the illusion of safety. But my brother invaded me there, too, moving in on me one morning while my mother sipped her coffee in the kitchen and read the morning news.

He was kneeling beside me in his underwear with his finger inside my underwear, poking inside the folds of my vagina. My underwear was pushed to the side, and there for all the world to see was a burst of dark hair and my brother's finger wedged inside me.

Someone in a writing class once asked us when it was that the world that we had built for ourselves had ceased to exist. While the other members of the class closed their eyes in thought, I had my moment in an instant. There on that bedroom floor I had known that anything good that was going to come of my life was going to have to come from inside of me. My parents could not be counted on to provide the simplest security. My brother was disturbed but would never get the help he was so desperately crying out for. If I were ever going to find a way out of that house, I could rely on only myself to find it.

When the abuse finally stopped (as it did shortly after that day), so did most of my illusions about the world. I withdrew into myself and into a fantasy world that I am sure contributes today to my being a writer of surreal/absurdist fiction. My adolescent life taught me what few barriers we have in life, how little our skin can protect us. In my fictional world, nothing is impossible.

I have asked myself, with the help of therapists and the like, why my parents did not provide me with a proper door. Why my mother insists that my brother's behavior was not unusual. "Boys are over stimulated," she says. I suppose she has no other choice but to believe that.

I have come up with some of the answers, and, like the abuse itself, they are painful. "We didn't realize you'd be so affected by all of that," my mother says, as if she'd believed I had been a piece of wood and not a child.

I have battled panic attacks for most of my life, since before I was thirteen, although they certainly intensified after the abuse. It wasn't until I was twenty and in the throes of a major depression that I found a word to describe the disorientation I often feel with my body, especially during panic. *Depersonalization*, a feeling of one's body not belonging to oneself, a word that certainly describes the facts of my adolescence. I suffer from a panic disorder, which is treated with a combination of medication and therapy and for the most part remains at bay, like my memories of the abuse. Occasionally these memories surface (though they are never really gone, only more muted at times than others), and I go through bouts of crying and depression and back into therapy, which helps me to realize how sane I really am.

Most importantly, I have become a writer, and although my fiction deals with surreal and absurd elements, it mirrors the bizarre nature of my adolescence, which, until now, I have not had the courage to write about. Learning to find words to match the feelings is what has saved me. *Incest. Abuse.* They are ugly words, but I have taught myself to say them—just as I have taught myself not to deny the feelings, not to be trapped in that room without a door. Writing has become my door, a way out of my pain, a way into myself. I can lock that door now if I choose to, or I can leave it open. But I can no longer leave it hanging there on its frame, as if there were no need for protection. It is my way into salvation; it is my only way out.

*I wish to acknowledge that Frances Louis is not my real name. Because my first novel has recently appeared and increased my visibility, I have become concerned about the possibility of family members coming upon it. Although I am willing to discuss these incidents in graphic detail, painful as they are, my family (like most) continues to live as if nothing has happened. Because I am not yet prepared to deal with the consequences of their having discovered this publication, it is for their protection, and perhaps for mine, too, that I am withholding my identity.*

# Daughter
Nancy

Born, into hurt and abandon,
an intense fear and hatred
where love should have been.
The hollowed out figure,
the cardboard prop
she called mother, had
no power to protect her daughter,
no courage to save,
no eyes to see,
her daughter.
Her only, precious one.
The one who was raped by her husband
    fondled by her father
    molested by her son.
The rage, it grew, it grew
flamed and fanned by passing years,
'til the daughter becomes a mother.
She learns to love.
She loves with a fierceness and
protectiveness of a lioness.
If any man touches her daughter,
offends, curses, or hurts
her daughter,

## Daughter

an anger, a fearful anger awaits
that rages redder than blood,
engaging a fury that
embroils her brain
severs reason and logic
scorching cinders
of painful, hot light,
to ignite the umbilical cord
that never is cut.
And the mother, who was a daughter,
in a momentous transfiguration
—a killer, murderer, butcher
willing and bloodthirsty
for her daughter's tormentor,
her daughter,
her only, precious one.

The ferocious mother remembers
    the vacant blue eyes
    the stillness of emotion
    on a smooth, impassive face.
The fissure cracks deeper,
With the full knowledge of betrayal.
And the anger bubbles and seeps
upon the wretched, cracked surface,
thus arming her, anointing her
for every battle ahead.

For her daughter,
her only, precious one.

# Graveyard

Christine Anne Pratt

The "Graveyard" matched my mood when I was twenty-four—flat, depressed, melancholy. I used to sit in this particular graveyard. I found its combination of beauty and quiet consoling.

# Enough Said
Carolyn

So I go to group. I sit. I talk. I go each week. This is the work I need to do.

I read Ellen Bass. I get a ticket in advance to hear Laura Davis speak. I do the work I need to do.

I go to my therapist appointments. I have become friends with her receptionist. I bring my usual cup of coffee. I am tired of the work that should be done.

My life is no different than others. I am not fire and hell to be around. I go to work. I take mental health days when I should. I know the jargon—understand the dynamics—master the psychobabble. What else do I need to do?

So my brother decided to play games. He was always precocious. Games supposedly harmless and mutual. I have always known that these games were played. My childhood was not so different. Strip Poker . . . Truth or Dare . . . My parents go to parties. The games begin.

touch this    touch that    rub this    rub that    LOOK    look Look

## Carolyn

down there
Look Look  Touch  Touch  Rub  Rub
As I rub, white grey stuff comes out              I look down
this is weird

So my alarm clock goes off. He set it for 5:30 a.m. He told me to wear my flannel nightgown. Light blue—no lace—lace itches me. No, don't wear your pajamas, wear your nightgown. I wear my nightgown. My alarm buzzes. I go downstairs. This is all part of a new game. I'm not sure what it is called. I walk into his room. He is awake. I wonder if his alarm went off when mine did. He moves over. I can have half his pillow. How nice. I get under the covers. He rubs with my hand. Rubs against my flannel nightgown. I look at his clock. 5:41. 5:42. 5:43. He rubs more. More of him on more of me. 5:54. 5:55. 5:56.      Dad's alarm will go off at 6:00.
I say 5:58. He takes his pillow back. Arranges my nightgown. Gets the gook off it. Closes his eyes to sleep. I walk into the kitchen. Get some juice. Carry the glass upstairs. Each morning my father asks me what I am doing up so early. It is summer vacation—remember you don't have to go to school unless you want to; better yet, you can go to work for me—a regular joke between us.
I say I am just thirsty. I wanted a drink.

So we go to New York for the next summer. Stay with Grace and Max. Don't call me Grandma—it makes me feel old—call me Grace. If I call her Grace, I should call him Max. We stay with Grace and Max. Two bathrooms. One is theirs. One is ours. I take a shower. He says I am hogging all the water—wasting all the water. Whatever it is I am doing I shouldn't be doing it. Whatever it is he says I am doing. He decides it is his turn to shower.
My time is up.

# Enough Said

He slides open the door. He gets in. Shampoo in my eyes. I close them. Move, you're in the way. I move. I close my eyes more tightly.
Move he says.   Nowhere else to move.   Move he says.
Press my eyes tighter. He moves next to me to press tighter. On my leg. It keeps moving.
I just want to get the shampoo out.

Time to go home. Summer is over. Get to the airport early. I sit next to the window. He sits by the aisle. Move I say. No. Move I say. He moves. I go to the bathroom. He goes to the bathroom. Wait I say. No. The bathroom has this strange grey light. It has this strange smell. I can't go in front of him. I want to get out. No. He can go in front of me. He goes. This is strange. There must be people waiting. The grey light makes it look darker grey. Dark grey stuff comes out. I still can't really figure it out. He goes again. Fine. It sticks to my stomach. Pull down my shirt. The movie is about to start. I'm embarrassed to walk out. Occupied—Vacant.

So I think it all was for five years. Maybe four. I should know how long it lasted.
I don't know for sure.   There should be more.

So I write this.   They tell me there is more to write.   How do you really feel.
I don't know for sure.   There should be more.

I look back over the words.   Once. Twice. Again  again  again.
I suppose I should look again. These things can always use more work.
I don't know for sure.    That is all.
Work that needs to be done.

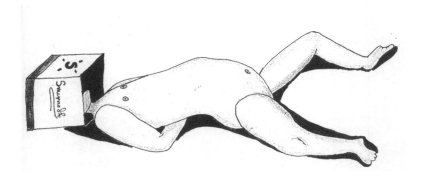

# #56 Ashamed

C.B. Clinton

When I entered therapy for what seemed to be the hundredth time, I knew there was something terribly, terribly wrong, but I didn't know what. In conjunction with therapy, I started to draw, and the images that emerged made me aware that I felt trapped in a box. As my body remembered my past, my drawings began to reflect the intensity of my abuse. That's when my healing began.

# #15 Boxed

C.B. Clinton

# The Therapist's Hope
Catherine Swanson

Carefully he laces the fingers
of his two hands together,
squeezing them tightly into a fist,
to demonstrate the dilemma—

> That the brother who taught love
> also taught terror,
> and the two,
> seared together in the mind
> of the girl, so young
> that she could not distinguish
> between *the affection of him,*
> who tousled her hair,
> taught her Beethoven and Brahms,
> all the rules of hockey,
> how to imagine wildly
> and laugh unencumbered,
> when no one else
> had time to look at her,
> and *the anger of him,*
> who invaded her sheets at night
> with a burning iron rod
> between her legs
> and the weight of twenty anchors.

Then slowly pulling the fingers
of his two hands apart,
he demonstrates the weld
broken.

# Breath

Susan Fredericks

At the Mink Creek Campground
lavatory, Margaret tore off
the last calling card
from the Support Center
Against Domestic Violence
and Sexual Assault.

While her parents hiked
toward the eastern mountains,
one fading behind the other
in the dusk, she planned to ask
advice. Weeping wouldn't matter
where no one could trace her,

tell her parents and bring
them to a greater grief
than her brother's life
had already delivered.
Margaret studied the number,
folded the card in her hand

## Susan Fredericks

and felt her jeans pocket
for the quarter saved
from the video game in Bath
when it had rained so hard
her parents apologized,
said they didn't remember

a summer so cold and wet.
With her back to the trail
and the family tent,
she read the three rows
of instructions three times,
punched in the numbers

holding back the breath
she could not use for words.

    *The teenage girl in this poem does not speak of her experience until her parents have both died and cannot be hurt by the knowledge of what their son has done. When she is able to find the words, this poem comes out of her. Next she is able to tell a therapist she has sought out for this purpose. Several months later, she tells her husband. Since therapy, she has had extremely limited communication with her brother. The abuse she experienced as a teenager defined her actions and haunted her for years.*

# Dirty Words
NíAódagaín

### 1.
Growing up
in my Mother's house
dirty words
weren't allowed

"I'll wash your mouth out
with soap
if I hear that again"
her threat, a beacon
throughout my childhood
helping me to navigate
the turbulent sea
of moral right and wrong

"stupid," "jerk," "retarded"
flung at a sibling
to inflict hurt
transformed my mother
into an avenging Angel
smiting, with her fierce
admonishment,
all evil notions
from one's soul.

## NíAódagain

Grown up now
far from my mother's house
my conflict, one of
seeking retribution

I want to know, Mother,
did you ever wash out
his mouth
and eyes
and hands
for the sins they
committed?

   2.
Will you do it now,
Mother
will you rub him so clean
that the light of God
shines in his eyes
shimmers from every inch
of his skin
down to the tip of his
swollen penis
which, at the moment
of his salvation
bursts...

Showering
flowers
red, gold, orange
flowers
blue, violet, magenta
flowers
flowers
and nothing more

but flowers.

# Little Blue-Eyed, Dark-Haired Italian Girl

Nancy Lee

Little blue-eyed, dark-haired Italian girl.
Standing at the curb in Yonkers
on a hot July day.
Struggling to understand.
Striving to be a good girl.
Wanting, desperately, to be loved.
Little blue-eyed, dark-haired Italian girl.
Trying to make sense of big brother's touch
and the odd feeling he stirs inside her.
Broken,
Drowning,
Crumbling,
Lost.
Little blue-eyed, dark-haired Italian girl.
All you know is
death, hatred, chaos,
incest.
All you know is terror.
Little blue-eyed, dark-haired Italian girl.
Now a woman.
Strong, determined, successful,
but
broken,
still.

# Why I Wake in the East While You Sleep in the West

*After the primitive Rhineland myth*
*"Sister Sun and Brother Moon"*

## Jennifer Corse Simon

You came to me
after my father told me,
*bank the fires*
*and sleep.*

Deep inside the cave
you padded and slipped
between the skins
to meet me at the

Center of creation.
So many times we lay,
belly cupping belly,
I had to know your face,

Though Father urged,
*keep the fires low.*
I blackened each
palm in the fire's

## Why I Wake in the East While You Sleep in the West

Cold bed and waited.
I took you to me,
my hands on your back.
You stole away

Before I rose in light.
That evening, as I
walked slowly home,
I saw you, Moon,

With our father's kiss
upon your head.
I turned to watch
you go, dear brother,

Only to find the impress
of my own desire
on your broad, shining
shoulders.  Now, each

Night as you rise
blotting out my slow burn,
I run to the earth's dark side.
We climb the same

Track of sky—all that's
left between us of this love
that I refuse,
that you pursue.

## Jennifer Corse Simon

*I came across this myth in Joseph Campbell's* Primitive Mythology, *(volume I of the* Masks of God *series). At the time (summer of 1986), I had just come to full realization of the abuse that I had suffered at the hands of my brother. The myth seemed the perfect vehicle for the grief and confusion I felt. Today I would say that the mutual desire expressed in the poem does not characterize the incestuous relationship between us. The age difference (nearly six years) and the coercion he used places the responsibility for the abuse squarely on his shoulders. Yet the poem expressed for me the loss of all relationship to my brother at that time. However, in the time elapsed as this anthology has evolved, my brother and I have found ways to heal and be a family once more. It is possible to forgive.*

# Section Three: Shattering Silences

Action Girl #6, Scorch, age 8.

# Untitled

Portrait 50" x 38" charcoal, acrylic paint, markers

C.B. Crowe

This drawing is a culmination of work dealing with the anger toward my three older brothers for taking away my childhood, betraying me, and for forming and exacerbating my feelings of worthlessness. I have worked very hard at overcoming the effects of molestation and have found through creativity the ability to release my anger in a positive manner.

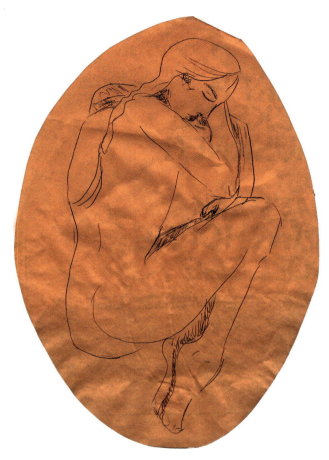

# The Sleeping Woman
Christine Anne Pratt

In my twenties, I hardly thought of myself as a woman, but drawing this picture gave me a feeling of safety, peace, and reassurance. It is also a self-portrait of the woman inside waiting to be awakened, to be born.

# Out of the Muck

Judy Stein

# The Action Girls

Risa Shaw

**B**orn of clay, tiny leather jackets, Barbie dolls, Ken dolls, popsicle sticks, magic markers, found objects, and the inspiration of a bunch of incredible women, the Girls (as we fondly refer to them) are incest survivor action figures.

Somebody had to make them.

Action Girl #3, Celtic Girl, age 14.

Action Girl #4, Bones, age 5.

# Creating Bugle
## Tessa Katz

Bugle is the announcer who blows the trumpet and stops the incest. She carries that bugle with her as her power object, her "don't mess with me" object. Bugle is fierce with her "back off!" face, and will not be silenced. She will continue blowing that trumpet if anything happens to her or anyone else. It is the badge she carries with her from the incest.

Making Bugle was a concrete embodiment of what I did to stop the abuse, and what I am proud of. She is an illustration of my story, which is laced with anger and confusion, especially in light of the fact that my brother now has mental health problems (paranoid schizophrenia). I got the incest to stop. I was six or seven years old and we were at a huge family gathering. In the middle of the celebrations I stood up and said, "By the way, do you know what my brother's doing to me...." There was shocked silence. The abuse never happened again, and it was never mentioned again.

Action Girl #1, Bugle, age 7.

# Scream

Michelle

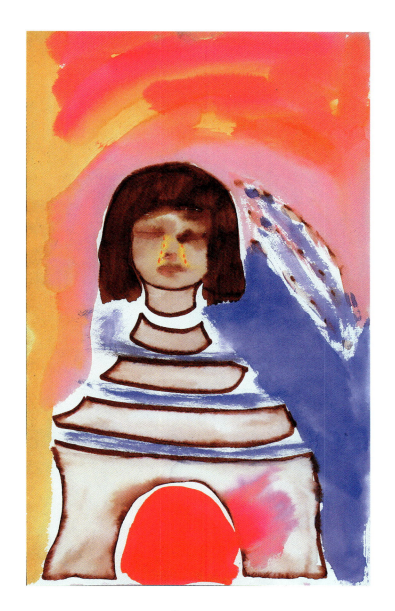

# Fragmented
Michelle

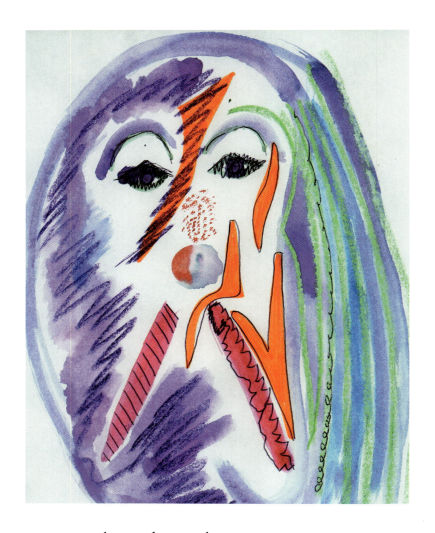

# Speak Clearly
Michelle

# Footsteps on the Stairs
Risa Shaw

"WHAT?!" His eyes are filled with horror, anger, and fear. The word "rape" has different meanings for the two of us. Maybe that's because I am on the verge of coming to terms with the reality of more than 15 years ago. It took me years before I could even think of the concept applied to myself and many more before I could speak it out loud. Now I am saying it in my everyday tone of voice, matter of factly.

Indeed it has happened. And after years of it being buried, my brother has no warning that it is to be brought up from its grave. How can he come to terms with it? Not in the same way that I have or ever will. Those experiences were not the same for the two of us.

Now, I am bringing it up. And not in a submissive manner. He has no control of this situation. After 28 years of manipulating, it comes quickly, but he has no forewarning. Even in his wildest nightmares, he would not have produced that moment. Or the scene of the next six days. The script was written 15 years before.

With the words spoken and his gaze upon me, he is flustered, but only for a fraction of a second. Denial is next, though his eyes yield to his deep-seated fear. There is anguish there, too, and for the rest of the week he remains guarded.

He cannot believe what I am saying. "It didn't happen." At least not in the way that I am describing it. Our recollections are too different. (Not that I am wrong, but he certainly doesn't remember those things—those disgusting things that I am accusing him of, even though the accusation is not in my voice. For him, it is in the words I have chosen.) I am just telling the truth, what it was like for me. "Rape and incest are terrible things. Things that happen to friends or strangers. But certainly not what happened between you and me." That is what his words, body, and eyes are telling me.

To him, I am not "wrong," but I must not be remembering things accurately. He claims he never would have done such a thing. And even if he had, Mom would have heard us because she was such a light sleeper. And she didn't hear us, so those things did not happen.

Don't I realize that being male means he knows exactly when he lost his virginity? He knows it wasn't until years later, and it wasn't with his sister. He tells me this — as though losing your virginity and being the perpetrator of rape falls into the same category for him.

He says we never did anything that we both didn't agree to. How could I have "disagreed" when I felt totally intimidated, scared to death of my big brother, and so ashamed that I wanted to bury myself alive? How was I to know whether or not his threats would be carried out?

He talks about some terrible cases of rape and incest that have happened to friends of his; how disgusted and incensed those make him. I wish that he could take those feelings and multiply them ten million times. Then he would have a better idea of how I feel every day of my life.

He talks about how terrible "those things" are and how he would never do anything "like that" to anyone, especially his sister. Funny how shared experiences can be twisted and seen as completely different entities depending on one's perspective.

At first, he tries to be nice. He wants to know if he can hug me. We are civil to each other, but I do not allow him to touch me. It is the first night of Chanukkah, and the family is together. Still, our eyes meet, and the energy stings. I am glad for the large number of people around. That means there is plenty to do, plenty of distractions. It also means that I do not have to sit in the same room with him while we eat dinner. This is lucky for all of us because I probably could not keep down even the chicken soup.

He questions me and pleads with me from the beginning. "Who knows?" "When did you tell them?" "What did you tell them?" "Why did you tell them?" "Don't tell anyone else, please." He always adds "please," at least for those first couple of days. Don't I realize that if I tell anyone else in the family, it will only be destructive for him, and toward him? I shouldn't do it.

But I do it. I am ready to explode because of the isolation, the self-blame, the craziness that I feel. I can't be with my family and pretend anymore. No longer am I willing to be an accomplice to pretending that the incestuous rape never happened. No longer am I willing to protect my brother. His actions have had a detrimental effect on essential parts of my ability to trust, respect, and be intimate. No longer will that destruction be allowed to continue.

Three days later, we talk again. When he learns that I have told our entire family, he says, "I am disappointed in you." He repeats those words over and over again. He is sitting very upright in a chair at the dining room table. I am sitting across from him. As he says those words, his body becomes rigid, his arm positioned carefully on the table, and his eyes lock in my gaze. His lips are tight. Controlled. His anger burns, but it does not touch me. It is apparent to both of us that he no longer holds any control over me.

He makes no effort to speak to me the following and last two days. His eyes carry an angry glare. That happens when the situation is charged and the tables have been turned. I am not used to KNOWING that I am right. He isn't either. He never raises his voice. He doesn't even pound his fist on the table. He just shakes his head. I easily could feel sorry for him. He is not in a pretty place. Not with himself or with his family. Everyone knows the long-kept secret. But I don't feel sorry for him. I feel proud of myself for my courage. It isn't easy. It has never been easy before, and it will not be easy in the future.

My brother's actions interfere with my life every day. I don't want his apologies. I want him to acknowledge and accept what he has done. I want the nightmares and mistrust to leave me alone. I want a guarantee that no one will ever have to go through this kind of hell again. But as long as people continue to deny the existence of incestuous rape, it will not stop. Those reminders my brother has left with me will never disappear. The rage will never leave me.

*I wrote this piece one day in January of 1985, just after I spoke to my family about the incest. Making the decision to talk to each of them may be the scariest thing I have ever done; actually talking to them, the second scariest. Both are undoubtedly two of the best things I have ever done.*

*Acknowledging the rage meant beginning a process of no longer turning that rage in on myself. It has taken years to realize the necessity of that process, and figure out how to recognize what turning it in on myself looked and felt like. Then, how and where else to direct it. Directing it in the appropriate places and at the appropriate people has been a challenge as well and continues to be, especially when I see the same power dynamics being played out in present time. I have hurled many an egg at many a tree and stockade fence. The crash is fantastic. Dart boards also come in handy, and punching bags. Writing the anger, the tirade, the rant and speaking it out loud, loudly, and over and over again, to say, to yell, to purge from my body what needs to be said, does wonders.*

# anger provoked
Meikil Berry

i want him out of here
away from my space     my earth
he should have his own planet
or even farther away
with his own kind

why don't you disappear?
become atomic and explode
unravel at the seams
disintegrate by lightning
get swallowed and shared in
equal parts by a tidal wave, tornado, hurricane, monsoon, earthquake,
    volcanic eruption

he should be shackled and stoned outside the city walls, burned at the
    stake, flogged,
whipped, guillotined, castrated, raped, mass murdered, tarred and
    feathered, lynched,
infected with malaria, kidnapped, stampeded by wild elephants with
    diarrhea,
used as shark bait, strapped with dynamite then ignited

he should never be loved, nurtured, comforted
he should never feel contentment, safety, or peace
he should never have family and friends

he should never see patience, generosity, or loyalty
he should never experience tears of joy, hope, pride,
dignity, self-esteem, orgasm, confidence, laughter, a good meal,
a cool breeze on a hot summer's day, a late night swim, lemonade,
    sunshine,
falling stars, rainbows, flowers, ice cream, candy, steamed crabs,
    apples and oranges,
a good night's sleep, trust, respect, admiration, romance, achievement,
    or birthdays

he should always experience The Great Flood,
The Great Depression, The Great Potato Famine,
assassination, suicide, homophobia, cholera, apartheid, poverty,
crucifixion, alienation, incarceration, incapacitation, incineration,
separation from limb to limb

he should be a paraplegic, obese, anorexic, leper with muscular
    dystrophy and cancer of
the brain, liver, stomach, and testicles

no he should have no testicles

he should be a sightless, soundless, voiceless, touchless genius
    Vietnam vet

he should be thrown from a moving train
out of an ascending plane
off the golden arches

he should bungee jump without a cord

## anger provoked

he should be perpetrated, abused, misused, mistreated, denied, brow beat, starved,
suffocated, constipated, regurgitated, squashed, pistol-whipped, kicked, spat on

he should never be happy, satisfied, blessed, understood, free, or forgiven

and hopefully he never will

# Confrontations
## Tanya Garig

The first one
was physical.

Your hand on my breast,
my hand wrapped around
a hard rock glass crashing
down on your knuckles,
once, twice, three times,
until you realized the extent
of my determination to stop you,
or die trying.

This one is verbal—

poetry rearranging the blame
in my head and
erasing the shame
from my heart.

Dear brother Jim,

# Confrontations

The memory of your touch
E X P L O D E S  in my brain.
I have to remind myself
things are different now.

These words are my POWER.

As you read them,
I want you to think
about who else might read them.
When you hear someone whisper,
I want you to wonder
if they are whispering about you.

I want the memory of your touch
to E X P L O D E  in **your** brain
and ricochet through **your** heart.

This one is justice—poetic justice,
rearranging the blame
in **your** head—
engraving the shame
on **your** heart.

# My Brother
Blanche Woodbury

My brother lives in a box of cigars.
Each day every day
he lifts the lid to peek at the world
and hopes the world won't notice.
Bristles grow on his face and throat.
He smells, fears soap.
He never throws his loose hairs away
but carefully keeps them, dirty and dark,
in the teeth of a green plastic comb.

Long ago he spent years committing incest.
I survived but we never mention it.
He's thirty-five now and still lives with our mother.
My favorite joke when I visit is to talk
of the time I stabbed his thigh with a fork
and sent him screeching around the table
for ruining my first perfect crayoned picture.
We pretend to laugh and the scar
does not go away.  Migraine headaches
take me back to the fork, to the fort
he built under cool pines
where he wouldn't let me visit
unless I would…and I did.

## My Brother

Now he does his best to repel.
He rots his teeth, sucks his cigars,
growls and belches and gets fat.
Each night every night
he grows a little smaller inside.
One morning my mother, weeping,
may find he's flickered out at last,
a tiny gray heap in an ashtray.
I'll visit, leave the jokes behind,
bring instead a perfect crayoned picture
to wrap around his coffin.

## Blanche Woodbury

*I would like readers to know that, with the help of a good therapist, almost half a decade after I wrote the poem, I made a bridge to my brother as our mother was dying. He is the one who has suffered the most (with the exception of my migraines, that is, which I'm pretty sure are in part a result of the "secrets and silences" of so many years), and I have learned that just as sometimes it is much more painful to be the leaver rather than the left in a love partnership, often it is the victimizer rather than the victim who goes through the most hell in guilt and remorse, torturing self in deep, unmitigable ways. I will never forget the conversation I seemingly calmly (but in terror) initiated with my brother in 1984 after our not having spoken directly to each other since 1961. I did the forbidden: I spoke directly of the incest. The result? I saw the decades' tension rush out of his body in a deep breath, and the nod of his head as he acknowledged the truth gave me wings to let the words continue. When our mother died 2 1/2 months later, we were able to work together on the funeral arrangements and the sorting of her possessions. Since then he has called me long-distance every Sunday night, as my mother used to do, just to talk, check in with each other, share complaints, and, as we both could with our mother, laugh.*

*Oh—one other note: not until 1983 could I bring myself to tell my best-friend-for-21-years of my family secret. How did I do it then? I read this poem aloud in a reading I was giving in a bookstore, in which she was in the audience. Afterwards she came up to me and said heartfully, "I always wondered what was wrong between you and your brother."*

*If I had not first written the incest poems (I believe made possible by the empowerment engendered by the annual summer Feminist Women's Writing Workshops) and then eventually found the courage to voice them aloud to audiences, I know I would never have been able to confront my brother and break that soul-killing silence. He and I are now family to each other as we never were for 32 years.*

# The Summons
Kathleen Fleming

The summons arrives on Friday afternoon just as Carl is pouring martinis from the shaker into four gold embossed cocktail glasses at the bar. The family room opens on the patio where his partner Richard and the wives are laughing. The ringing doorbell sends the collie racing around the house, and by the time the youngest son opens the door, the server is retreating to an old Dodge parked behind the other cars in the long driveway.

"Dad!" the boy yells, "this guy wants you!"

"Call off the dog, and it's 'There's someone to see you,' not 'this guy'—understand?" Carl swings the boy around, gripping his shoulder tight enough to make the boy stiffen against the pain as he nods.

Carl sets the shaker on the hall table and goes out. "Sorry about the dog," he says mildly, sizing up the young man in a fake tweed suit. Identifying him as a salesman, he stops walking toward him, pulls back his arm that was about to reach to shake hands, and puts it casually against his hip as he waits, his face flushed with an earlier drink and the exercise of grappling with his son.

"Mr. Carl Markells?"

"And you?" A faint smile curls out of sight before it surfaces. He could buy out fifty boys like this in an afternoon.

The stranger's voice blurs into his sleeve as his arm flips forward a long thin document and simultaneously a pen and another paper for Carl to sign.

Carl blanches slightly for a second, then remembers his partner's luncheon comment of several weeks before. "We may have some unpleasantness with Erickson before we're through—they think they can nail us for that substandard foundation crap, but they can't, so don't let it throw you if their attorney calls. Just call Simon and let him handle it. I already filled him in. We're clean." Carl checks the form, signs, flashes the sort of smile he saves for useless employees as he fires them, and turns back to the house. Footsteps behind him go down the driveway, a car door closes, an engine starts up and drones away.

"We're in need, real need," Terry calls from the patio. "Aren't we, Richard?"

"Speak for yourself," Richard says, slapping his wife's compact rear, and they all laugh.

"I'm here to save the day," Carl says, picking up the shaker, letting a full and open smile move across his face. "One at a time, Terry, rules of the game." He feels his body comfortably tall above her, comfortably aroused by her always present flirting. "I'll start the charcoal—god knows when the Macannineys will make it, right?"

"I'll give you a hand," Richard says. "I want to hear how Ray looked when you told him Henry had signed." The two men laugh knowingly as they walk.

"We have bad news from Erickson, I guess."

"How so? I thought that all blew over."

"We just got served." Richard stops walking. Carl glances back to see if the women are listening before he speaks again. "I left it in the house—a summons and list of complaints."

"No kidding? Where is it?"

"On the bar. Go check it out while I light this stuff, and I'll come see—no sense worrying Mack when he comes."

Carl bends to pour a new layer of briquettes over old ashes and pours the fluid carefully, watching its golden oiliness wash into the crevices between the shining black hard coals. He pulls his silver lighter from his pants, flicks it on, lowers it steadily until the tongue of flame hovers almost against the dampened coal. He freezes it there, feeling the tension in his groin match his arrested motion. For a long moment, he savors the suspense and then flicks his hand downward and upward, leaving behind a spurt of flame that flickers all the way across the barbecue bed and settles to what satisfies him as a lasting glow.

"Carl?"

He swings toward the house, alert. "Yeah?"

"This isn't from Erickson."

Relief is cut off by doubt. Who then? Something in Richard's voice. One of the kids? A stolen car? Drunken driving? A pregnant girl's irate father? Carl empties his glass in one gulp and goes into the house.

"One of the kids?"

"No. Here. You figure it. Hey, there's Mack. I'll go."

The summons is for him. Carl stares at the thick paper, deciphering the legalese. Court, State of Virginia? His mind is blank—no accounts in Virginia. I don't even know anyone in Virginia except Hildy, he thinks, then relief surges through him. The voices in the driveway are their friends. He is needed to make more drinks. The kids are all fine. It must be to be a character witness in her divorce, of course. To support her custody fight—something like that. Funny, he would've thought she'd stay with that lawyer husband. Not honest enough maybe. The kid had always been a little nutty that way. Or maybe he had too many women, and she couldn't relate to that. Everyone's not as sensible as Elise, he thinks, watching his wife coming to tell him to bring drinks. Even when Elise found out about the setup at the company's monthly conferences, she hadn't lost it. "No more of that," she'd said, and never wanted to know if she had won. So Hildy needs help—a notarized statement concerning her character should do.

Carl calls out, "Everyone settling for martinis? Except Mack. I know he has to have his scotch—everybody else?" And his eye, long trained to check out the fine print, catches the list of complaints, and he jerks his glance back up the page to where his name is branded: Defendant: charged with sexual abuse of a minor—on the premises—the old home address and the years.

"Carl, have you lost the ice?" Terry comes, laughing, through the door and puts ice in several glasses. Her face at forty-five is sharply delineated by dark eyebrows, deft mascara, lips drawn exactly right, Carl thinks—exactly right. He feels his own lips tremor—that pleasant unseen tremor that echoes his alert thighs as he grins at her, feeling a charge move up his arm as their hands meet around the glasses she is bringing for refills.

He thrusts the paper under the telephone book on the counter. "What shall I give you?" Carl asks, laughing down at her.

"What do you have?" Terry laughs back up.

"Anything you want, woman, anything you want."

"Pretty sure of yourself, aren't you?"

"You'd better know it."

"A martini on the rocks then."

They both laugh. For a second he thinks, some night I'll take her on for real. But Richard's familiar laugh comes through the door, and Carl knows he never will. Not his partner's wife. His rules are absolute, and one of them is to play fair with his partner. "Go see what Richard's laughing at," he says, handing her a double. "And then come find me, and I'll give you anything you want, honey, and more."

Terry blushes and giggles and goes back to the patio.

At the refrigerator, taking out the thick slabs of meat, Carl sees the words again. They make no sense to him, but the letters stand out clearly in his mind.

"INCEST: Charged with incest and sexual abuse of a minor." His hands on the trays cannot move. His fingers are clamped by cold to the steel. The sensation moves from the fingertips to the wrists to the arms to the armpits. He stares at the Coldspot letters before him. He stares. Between him and the world he owns, refrigerator, kitchen, house, yard, business, between him and the people he possesses, wife, children, partner, friends, neighbors, business associates, stands like an eye doctor's pinpoint of light the letters: COLDSPOT. But they are transformed—by too many martinis, he wonders for a mini-second and dismisses that easy save—to the single word—INCEST.

Carl uses the phone in the study. "Hey, Hildy, what's going on? This some kind of joke, eastern style?"

"No joke."

"What's this all about, kid?"

"I thought the list of charges was pretty clear."

"Are you for real?"

"Yes. At work I've handled a lot of child abuse cases, and I've decided to be a test case. I'm suing you for costs of therapy and compensation for harm, bodily and mental."

His voice is easy, condescending now, "Hildy, if you're in trouble, I want to help you. I'll send you money for the therapy. Tell me what you think would cover it, plus some extra, but take it easy, kid, you wouldn't want to hurt Elise and the kids, not to mention your own kids. Think a little about the consequences."

"Carl, I'm not into blackmail. I'll take some money for therapy costs. You owe me that, everything else aside. But that's not enough. Someone has to make a test case."

Circling, he comes in warily with another tone. "How are things going otherwise, Hildy? Your Christmas card sounded like you're working in a good place. We thought if you get a vacation this summer you might want to come out with the kids."

"No thanks, Carl. I don't think I want to talk in a friendly way with you anymore. I don't think I even want to have anything more to do with you, except in court. And I won't let my kids near you."

"Come on, Hildy. I don't know what you're into, but knock it off. Now, before somebody gets hurt."

"Maybe it's time somebody like you does get hurt, Carl."

"Don't you give a damn about anybody?"

"Yes, I do. I think there should be a test case. I think it might help to stop child abuse."

"Child abuse? Who's talking about child abuse?" His voice is rising now in a way it did when he was young, a way he cannot tolerate.

"I am. You molested me from the time I was seven years old until I was seventeen. That's ten years of child abuse. You are eight years older. That makes you past the age of reason when you began and twenty-five when you stopped because you got married."

"I never hurt you any. For Christ's sake, Hildy, kids fool around. You just don't remember how it was. We were just horsing around. I never hurt you any."

"You never beat me, if that's what you mean."

"Come on, you're making a mountain out of a molehill. We fooled around a little, that's all. You never screamed, you know."

"I couldn't fight you off, Carl. You used me. That's child abuse."

"That's crazy. That's a weird thing to say. We were just kids."

"I was just a kid. You went to war and came back and still used me. You had a habit—she laughs a rough laugh, "and I was it."

Carl clicks a switch in his head the way he does at work when he has to use two phones at once. His voice changes. "Never mind. Make an ass of yourself. Go ahead. Somebody's using you all right—women's libbers, lezzies, somebody. But deal me out, little sis. I'll give it to my attorney. He'll handle it. You're just making a stupid fool out of yourself."

"Maybe and maybe not. I've just had five years of therapy, and I think my head's pretty straight. You really messed me up. That's weird all right. You tortured me for years, big brother."

"Cut it out. Somebody put that in your head. You don't believe that."

"Did anyone ever torture you? Ever? Men like you shouldn't get off scot-free, you know? I want to set a precedent. Little girls should be safe in their own homes. We're not talking about dark streets at night. We're talking about safe neighborhoods and nice big brothers. That needs talking about, right out loud, in court."

He hangs up. Torture. *He is at summer camp. Ten. After swimming, naked, he takes a dare and lowers himself down the ladder in an old cistern behind the camp. The big kids throw a garter snake in on him and slam down the boarded top. He shakes off the snake in a violent spasm. The light is gone. In the blackness there is nothing but sweat wriggling down his skin. Pebbles and dirt ping the water far below. He cannot see the opening above. A scream blocks up his throat. His hands clench the rotting sides of the ladder, the wet wood softening in his grip. From far, far away, their laughter is running down his flesh, trickling, slithering like the quick passage of the thrown snake.*

Carl walks outside and puts the steak on the grill. Richard is coming toward him. He empties someone's glass, left on the patio. Did Richard read the little print? Reject. Reprogram. Big print? Little print. Big print.

"Hey, you're swallowing kind of fast, aren't you?" Richard lays his hand on his arm.

"Comes of the biggest deal of the season. That's what we're here to celebrate, isn't it?

"Um."

"What's your dark look about? We're on top."

"Are you okay, Carl?"

"Sure, I am." What had Richard read? Sister. Sister. What had he read? "My sister's in trouble. Dirty divorce case. I may have to give her a hand."

Extradition laws? No. Unreal. She wouldn't go through with it. Couldn't. You don't say things like that. Not to anybody. Couldn't persuade a judge. Kid stuff. Say out loud to Richard, say it carefully, "Loony, that girl. She's losing it." Already told him she's too good for that moron. Too honest. Too truthful. Screw that. Say nothing. Rich won't ask. Good old Richard. I could have Terry any time. He trusts me. "You can trust me, Rich, you know that?"

Richard hits his back, hard. "I know that, partner."

The smoke curls up around the steak. The two men stand, watching it. "Let's replenish the fountain of youth," Carl says.

"Maybe you should taper off."

"Don't blow the whistle on me, coach."

"You're letting that crazy summons thing total you. Let's call Simon."

"Right."

Carl walks carefully behind Richard, left, right, left, right, until they are inside. Has he read it? Does he know? The bed, thirty years ago. Scraps of smuggled mags. *I next worked for a baker, a hairy little runt. I had to quit that job because he begged to suck my cunt. National Geographics*, smudged, rubbed thin—naked women, black bodies dancing, stretching, bending. Groin throbs, throbs: grab the kid, shove it, ram it in there where her thighs lie together, hot and soft.

It just took a minute. God, kids are quick. She just lay there. She never yelled, Carl thinks as they go into the den, walls spinning. Christ, too much gin too fast. Stupid. "Richard. Is the steak okay?" Acrid smell.

"The steak's okay. Mack's doing it."

"Good. That's extravagantly generous of Mack."

"Sit down, Carl."

"Can't. Have to go thank Mack. Extraordinary good friend, Mack."

Richard grabs his arm and pushes him into the chair. "Stay here, Carl. I'm getting you coffee."

"Richard?"

"Yeah?"

"Richard?" Which out loud and which allowed? Which outlawed? Carl laughs. "Richard, out loud is the opposite of outlawed, right? And in-law is allowed. Correct?"

# The Summons

Richard hands him a cup of coffee. "Swallow it."

"Before dinner?"

"Right."

He swallows. "Nothing to it. Kid stuff. Believe me."

"Sure. Lots of kids mess around. Let me see it again."

Carl goes to the refrigerator, opens it, closes it, studies the COLDSPOT. He looks around and takes the summons out from under the telephone book and takes it back to Richard. He extends it to him at arm's length and watches him as he reads.

"Carl, she can't make this stick. Call Simon. He'll handle it."

Dialing. "Rich, you know how kids play around, like kicking shins under the table or making your brother giggle while he drinks so he gushes his milk out all over everything? Simon? My sister's losing it, Simon. There's a subpoena." Carl looks around for a glass and holds it out to Richard. "For Christ's sake, Rich, Simon put me on hold. Here, fill this."

"I don't think so. You've been chugalugging doubles a little fast. Want me to talk to Simon?"

"No, I can do it."

"Then I'll take a leak."

Carl grips the receiver. He lays the summons on his knee. Hildy's voice still curls like wisps of smoke out of the receiver and around his head. Unreal. It was nothing, what they did. Even Elise sometimes sucks me off, he thinks, and the women at conferences. He puts his hand in his pocket, feeling himself, as he remembers one girl's tongue.

Simon's tired office voice cuts in on him. For one long second, Carl sees his sister's lips, locked shut, and thinks, with dreamlike clarity, her eyes were always closed.

"Okay, Simon. Here's the thing. There's nothing to it, you understand? What we did as kids was play doctor, in a way. All kids do that. The stress of getting a divorce, or I don't know. My sister's hallucinating."

Simon's sharp voice cuts in, wanting specifics.

119

## Kathleen Fleming

"All right, all right. I got a subpoena and a list of complaints. It reads like this." Carl reads the words mechanically, then answers a few questions. "Right. Of course not. No one. They're dead, both of them. She never told. Not that there was anything to tell."

Simon's legal voice takes over, lifting from Carl all recollection, all need to remember. Carl's hand relaxes on the receiver. He can focus again on the patio where Mack is carrying the steaks to the table. Couples drift there, glasses in hand. The wide lawn stretches to the pool, the pool glows with underwater recessed light. Beyond the pool, the shrubs with their dark glossy green separate the world outside from their laughter, their linked arms, the sure voice on the phone.

"Yeah. I've got it. Deny. Statute of limitations should stop her. But if not, after that I just deny it all."

Simon goes on, reassuring him, calls it acting out, a wild long shot. Carl echoes his last words, "Yeah, as much chance as a snowball in hell. Thanks, Simon. Appreciate it."

Richard is beside him, waiting.

"Okay. That's it. No need to mention this, right?" Carl pours himself some gin and drinks it neat.

Richard does not try to stop him. "Hell no. What do you take me for?"

"Let's go, buddy." Carl grabs Richard's arm with his right hand, driving his thumb against the nerve center opposite the biceps on the inside of his arm. Richard winces.

"Remember that one from seventh grade?" Carl laughs, letting go, and hits the arm with a familiar punch.

Richard laughs, returns the punch.

Terry's voice comes high across the lawn. "Hey, you two! No more calls, no more work. We're skinny-dipping after brandy. You game?"

"Like the market—nothing like a plunge to make it rise again!" Mack's heavy laughter crosses the pool with the little waves that lap to silence at the shallow end.

Carl passes Elise, carrying out a big bowl of salad. She puts her hand on her husband's arm. "Were you on the phone with Hildy?"

"Yeah. She's in the middle of the divorce."

"Poor kid. Did she sound all right?"

Carl stares at his wife. *He sees the salad drop to the patio, tomatoes splattering on the brick, lettuce fluttering in all directions, and Elise backing off from him. At the same second, he sees Richard leave the table, followed by Terry, with frightened eyes. He sees his children and their friends, laughing in a gang around the pool, suddenly turn, wrap themselves in towels, walk out of his house for good.*

The vision gone, Carl speaks, "I had a message at work to call her, so I did. Nothing special. I have a hunch she's losing it."

"Oh, I'm sorry, darling. Maybe I'll call her later. Maybe she should send the kids here while the court stuff goes on. Bring the wine, will you?"

"Right."

"It's that nice Beaujolais. I already opened it to let it breathe." Elise moves on toward the table.

Carl watches her a moment and then turns away from the table, away from the pool. Abruptly he breaks into a thick, cold sweat, feels it soak his shirt, his shorts. His whole body shivers, as he goes back into his house.

# Preface
## Judy Stein

I was sexually abused by my second oldest brother, from the age of 5 to the age of 20. Although I always had knowledge of his actions, it took years of intensive therapy before I was able to acknowledge that they were abusive and at the root of most of the dysfunction in my life.

Once I did recognize the abuse, I thought my brother surely would, too. He was now a practicing child psychiatrist. He must be confronted every day with the reality of what sexual abuse does to a child. How could he listen to his clients' stories, help them through their pain, and not recognize that he had been a perpetrator of similar pain? How did he reconcile the guilt this must engender?

I talked to him a few times about the abuse. He displayed a clinical interest, asked if it would help if he said he was sorry, but said he felt no guilt. As I began to feel more and more the extent of what I had lost in my life, because of his abuse, I wrote him an angry letter trying to detail this and asked him to come to a few therapy sessions with me as the one thing he could now do to try and make things right.

His response was that he was sorry for my pain, but he had more important priorities in his life at that point, mainly, a bitter and costly custody battle for his daughter that had been going on for years. He said he *would let* me *know if and when it would be convenient for him to come.*

A few years later, after my brother had at long last won his custody battle, I thought, OK, he has no more excuses, it's my turn now.

# Preface

*But still I heard nothing from him. In frustration, I wrote "Letter to the State Judicial System" as a therapeutic exercise. It was never really my intention to send it to the court, but I never completely ruled out the possibility either.*

*As my therapy continued, I became increasingly angry that I had to recover in a vacuum. I felt I needed some answers that I could get only by confronting my brother directly and judging for myself his response. Did he have any concept of what he had done to me? Was he doing it to his daughter?*

*I wrote my brother another letter, "What Do You Tell Your Daughter?" enclosing "Letter to the State Judicial System" as a not-so-veiled threat. After all the years of talking rationally to him, it was this angry threat that brought action. Within a month, we had therapy appointment times and he had airline reservations—everything in terms of "whatever I needed." I never sent the threatening letters to the governing agencies, but they did serve their purpose for me. Four months after the joint appointments, I terminated therapy.*

# What Do You Tell Your Daughter? A Letter to My Brother

Judy Stein

May 29, 1994

What do you tell your daughter as to why her aunt has no contact with her? Do you tell her that you hurt me very badly and that my avoidance has to do with you, not her? Do you explain anything to her, or do you just remain silent and let her think what she will?

What do you tell your lover, after these many years you have been together, about why you have no contact with this sister whom you purportedly adore? Do you tell her I'm very angry with you? Do you tell her why? Or do you remain silent as you have done with me all along?

What do you tell your sexually abused patients who want assurance that the abuse wasn't their fault and want to know how to deal with and confront their abusers, when you, as an abuser, have never taken responsibility for what you have done or tried in any way to make amends? Does that mean that you are still an abuser? How can you possibly counsel your patients with any understanding or empathy when you have shown no understanding of the damage you have done to me?

Dad said that when he asked you to tell him about your sexual abuse of me, you explained to him that you "just adored" me and even had a fantasy about donating a kidney to save my life. Is that a justification? An excuse? A defense?

Is it adoration for an 11-year-old boy to grope around his 5-year-old sister's vagina nightly when she's told him, in the only

# What Do You Tell Your Daughter?
## A Letter to My Brother

way she knows how at that age, that she doesn't want him to?

Is it adoration for that boy to lie naked on his bed on a weekend morning and insist against all his little sister's resistances and squeamishness that she touch his erect penis?

Is it adoration for an older brother to spot his little sister while she's learning to do handstands and, while she's hanging upside down, pull her body between his legs so it rubs against his penis?

Is it adoration for a medical student to stick his penis in his sister's vagina after he has experimented with sticking it in her anus, knowing full well it could cause an infection, which it did? I could go on.

**You are perverted if you think any of what you did had anything to do with adoration.**

You can talk all you want about "adoration" or donating a kidney to save my life, but in my eyes, all that does is point out what a fucking hypocrite you are. None of it means squat, when you haven't done one thing to help me heal from damage you caused. Even the best of intentions (which you did not have) would not excuse what you did, erase the damage, or change the outcome.

**Just because you might think you loved me does not make anything okay.**

At this point, we will **never** have a relationship until you take responsibility for what you did and acknowledge the lifelong damage and pain it has caused me. Given that you have not done this, I have no tangible reason to believe that you have changed, that you do indeed understand the impact of your abuse, and that you are not still doing similar things to your own daughter or your girlfriend's daughters or even your patients.

Simply admitting you did it is not the same as taking responsibility for doing it.

Following is a letter I wrote to the state court system after I heard you were awarded custody of your daughter. I have not yet decided whether to send it. I'm thinking of sending a copy to the Board of Psychiatry.

# Letter to the State Judicial System

Judy Stein

I understand that you just awarded custody of an adorable 10-year-old girl to a local psychiatrist. I think you should know that the same psychiatrist molested another young girl, his sister, for over 15 years, from the time he was 11 until he was well into his twenties. He did not stop his abusive behavior on his own volition. The behavior stopped only when his sister said "no more" and refused to be in situations where she was alone with him.

To this day, he has never taken responsibility for his actions or tried in any way to rectify the situation by helping in his sister's attempts at recovery.

Given this, I would be very concerned as to whether he realizes the lifelong ramifications and deleterious effects that child sexual abuse has on its victims, even though he purports to be a child psychiatrist who deals daily with abused children.

Therefore I would have strong reservations in awarding custody to someone who is an unrepentant child molester.

I worry for his innocent daughter who already may be a victim, I worry for the other two girls that live in his household, and I worry for his patients.

Sincerely,

The Sister

# Letter to the State Judicial System

*When asked to write a biography to accompany my contributions to this anthology, I found it very difficult. The dry facts about my life that one would typically expect to find in a biography seemed to have little relevance to the topic at hand and to the long and arduous healing journey I've been on. Besides, the person I would write about in such a biography is no longer me: she is the person I was before healing.*

*I break my life into three parts now, before healing, during healing, and after healing. The person I am now, after healing, would write a different biography. It goes like this:*

*I grew up the youngest and only girl out of four children. While my parents provided us with the material necessities of food, clothing, and the opportunities for a good education, they were too wrapped up in their own interests to give us the warmth, love, and attention we so sorely needed. Also, due to their own dysfunctions they were unable to set appropriate boundaries for us.*

*My second oldest brother, starved for the love and warmth he should have been getting from my parents, turned to his baby sister to get it. I, in turn, became very confused. The sexual contact my brother was having with me, that felt so icky and intrusive, was the only attention I was getting. I confused it with love, and as I grew older believed that letting people do things to me sexually was the only way to get love.*

*This was not the only effect of my brother's abuse. All the ramifications of that abuse are too numerous to name in this brief biography; suffice it to say, for the first 30 years of my life, I was not a whole person.*

*At the age of 33, I went into therapy for the third time. For five years, my life was nothing but therapy and healing, both for my body and mind. I did conventional psychotherapy, chiropractic, acupressure, massage, meditation, and yoga in an attempt to integrate the memories of my body with the rationalizations of my mind.*

*At the age of 38, I am just coming out the other side of that dark tunnel. Body and mind are much more integrated. I have boundaries. My body sets them for me by giving me signals, and I listen to them. It's called "trusting your gut." I have just started a wonderful, romantic love relationship with another woman that feels strong, nurturing, and healthy.*

# Preface
Patten O'Brien

  I turned 30 years old in January of this year. Shortly after my birthday, I received a letter from my eldest brother saying that he was saddened by the distance between us. He recognized that it was in large part his fault, apologized vaguely for the past, and said he would do whatever it takes to bring us closer together. In crafting a response, I wanted to be specific: specifically name his behavior and name my terms for reconciliation. I made many frustrating attempts that wandered off the point I wanted to make, got too emotional to feel firmly grounded, or left me feeling too vulnerable and exposed. Then I got the inspiration to name the abuse from my brother's perspective rather than mine, so that it became an admission rather than a confrontation. I wrote the first and final draft in 45 minutes.

  As I write this, I am very nervous because my brother has either just received my letter or will receive it in the next day or two. My mood in mailing the letter was remarkably calm and strong; now I am anxious because of the unknown.

# Writing a Wrong: Confrontation by Letter

Patten O'Brien

October 22, 1993

John:

You said you are willing to do whatever it takes to bring us closer together. Here's what it takes:

1. Find a therapist.
2. Tell your wife.
3. Tell Mom and Dad.

If you don't know what to say, here's how to start:

*When I was growing up, I sexually abused my sister Patten and my brother Andrew.*

*When I babysat for them, I taught them what they called The Babysitter Game. They felt each other out. I felt Patten out. I taught them to French kiss. I gave Patten a book by Jerry Rubin with lots of pictures of naked people in it. I told her I could hypnotize myself and then I would do anything she told me to. She told me to undress and stand like one of the men in the picture.*

*I let her touch my penis. I told her it felt better if she used her mouth. How did I know that? She was disgusted at the idea. This was in the house on Elm Street, so she was younger than 9. I am 6 years older than she is, so I couldn't have been older than 15.*

*I tucked Patten in at night in the house on Elm Street. We lay on her bed French kissing. I put her hand on my penis and my fingers in her vagina. We did this in the French provincial 4-poster bed with the*

## Patten O'Brien

*flowered canopy that my 3-year-old daughter now sleeps in.*

*I slept naked next to Patten at Grandma Smith's house.*

*In the house on Blair Road, I had my hand in Patten's pants while the whole family, even the dog, sat around watching tv. I was feeling her vagina and genitals for a long time. After, it burned when she peed.*

*In the house on Blair Road, I had Patten on her back on the floor in her room. I had her pants down around her ankles and knelt between her legs. I had my fingers up her vagina and on her cervix, and I asked her if I could rape her. She had dark pubic hair, so she must have been at least 12, and I was at least 18. Patten didn't even know what the word meant, and when she told Mom I had asked her if I could rape her, I denied it.*

*When Patten was molested by a stranger in the park, I denied it.*

*I probably learned to molest little girls from Bo Davidson, who lived across the street and molested Patten before I did. Maybe I helped Bo molest Patten. Maybe Bo molested me.*

*Although Patten has spent years in therapy alone, we have never dealt with this as a family. Now we can't avoid it, though, because Patten is afraid for my daughter's safety; Patten is getting married and everyone on her side at the wedding, including Andrew, has known for years that I am a rapist; and Patten and her husband will not be able to leave their children alone with me. Patten and her husband are forcing the family to deal with it; now it's a question of whether Patten and her husband will run the show or we all will contribute to the process.*

*Enough artifice. I need help.*

My fiancé and I will see you at Christmas. Here are the rules:

1. You don't seek me out. If I want to talk to you or write letters, I will let you know.
2. You don't initiate physical contact. No hugs, no kisses. If I want contact, I will let you know.

## Writing a Wrong: Confrontation by Letter

3. I don't want to be alone with you. You ask my permission before you come into a space where I am alone. If you don't, I'll scream.
4. No jokes. Your relationship with me is serious business. You are on probation.

Christmas is a test run. If it goes okay, I'll let you come to the wedding.

Patten

*To my amazement, within five days of receiving my letter, my brother saw a counselor and confessed to my parents. My parents called me right away to see if I was all right—18 years after the fact. They did not choose my brother over me, as I had feared they might. My father kept us all in triangulated communication throughout the crisis immediately following the revelation, and the whole family came together for a few hours on Christmas day. We did not discuss, or even acknowledge, the incest in that first meeting, but it no longer lurked in the corners of the house; anger no longer seethed beneath my every word. It was a new experience to see my brother on good behavior, to watch him follow my lead. I like the feeling.*

# After "Sorry"
Amy Blake

Oh brother.
Eight years past your last touch
You said, "I'm sorry."

If words could make a difference
      THE HATE.   THE FEAR.
      THE ISOLATION.
      THE PAIN.   THE DEPRESSION.   THE RAGE.
Would not have been the soldiers
In the war
I waged against myself.

Your words did not restore me
to myself.
Imprints of your hands, tongue, penis, the knife
remain etched in my soul.
Your words did not breathe life
into the me long dead.

My WARRIOR SPIRIT found
what you had left
abandoned.
My POWER grows in battle
My SELF-LOVE grows in the trenches
My JOY grows

# After "Sorry"

HEALING is my VICTORY
for not allowing
my journey to end
with your words.




*The most defining moment of my development occurred on a sweet summer's day toward the end of my fifth year. "In My Brother's Care" (page 17) describes the moment that is the beginning of continuous sexual exploitation by both of my brothers, two boys from the neighborhood, and a coach. Fighting the idea of myself as a sexual object at every twist and turn has been more of the battle for me than resolving any one incident. "After Sorry" is my experience of healing and how no one can give that to me. Even with the right words, all the work of healing is my work.*

*Brother-sister incest has been viewed as "child's play and harmless experimentation." That may be true for some but not for me. It took years for me to acknowledge that what happened to me was real—real abuse and real incest. This kind of abuse is not just about sick family dynamics. Our society values boys. Boys are encouraged in their sense of entitlement, and when they abuse their sisters, they do so for many reasons but mostly because they can. My hope is that as we see and hear about the pain, the damage, and the waste that this incest causes, we will be another step closer to ending this violence and living in a world that values our lives.*

# Women Shipyard Workers (Gdansk, Poland)
Charcoal on paper, 1984

## Ruth Trevarrow

This drawing is from a small photo in a newspaper. It was immediately imprinted on my brain; an image of solidarity and camaraderie with other women. I cannot count the number of times I have told my story of sexual abuse, only to find another woman say, "me too." What a club to be a member of; every time I am pained and relieved anew.

# Contributor Notes

**Sarah Elizabeth Barrett** has an M.A. in community/clinical psychology. She is an experienced educator, journal writing consultant, psychotherapist, and a survivor. She has presented workshops on sibling incest at national conferences, and has facilitated psychoeducational groups for sexual abuse survivors. In 1990 she organized and chaired a women's group which sponsored weekend retreats for survivors of child sexual abuse. In addition, she has edited a local child abuse prevention newsletter and a parenting column for area newspapers.

**Meikil Berry**. No biography.

**Amy Blake** is a survivor of childhood sexual abuse. As a therapist in private practice, she works with survivors and others on their healing. She is also a co-owner of A Woman's Prerogative Bookstore in Ferndale, Michigan.

**Carolyn** is a special education teacher who works with youth with autism. Previously, she directed a program that addressed sexual assault among people with disabilities. This is her first work to appear anywhere besides on scrap pieces of paper. "Enough Said" is also dedicated to her sister Tova, who is her closest ally, best friend, and fellow survivor.

**C.B. Clinton** is a 42 year old woman who lives with her son in Keene, NH. A few years ago C.B. began to use art and creative writing to recover her memories of her experiences of childhood sexual abuse and

## Contributor Notes

incest. During her healing process, C.B. says that she would become so involved in her work that the images she had created would sometimes shock her with their intensity. C.B.'s strong sense of spirituality has played an important role in her healing process, allowing her to become a healer of others. Her artwork has an emotive quality that draws the viewer in with its strength and power.

**C.B. Crowe** is a 45 year old Anglo lesbian. As an incest survivor, she has spent considerable time and energy dealing with the aftermath. Now, she explores the emotions of these experiences through her artwork. The combination of creativity and release help in the healing process.

**Kathleen Fleming**'s last novel, *Lovers in the Present Afternoon*, was published by Naiad Press. Her most recent short stories were in *The Romantic Naiad* and *Lesbian Bedtime Stories 2*. Retired from teaching, she walks the beaches and swims on Long Island, sometimes visited by her grown children and young grandchildren. She leads writing workshops for women and works in groups active against bias.

**Susan Fredericks** has a B.A. and M.A. in English and American Literature. She is married and has two children.

**Tanya Garig**. No biography.

**C. Gordon** is a poet and teacher who lives in Gloucester, Massachusetts. Her latest work has been published in the *Southern Poetry Review*. She has published two chapbooks with Folly Cove Books in Gloucester, MA 01930. The titles are *Two Girls on a Raft* and *When the Grateful Dead Came to St. Louis*.

**Mary Diane Hausman** was born and raised in the Texas hill country. She now resides on the East Coast where she writes,

## Contributor Notes

teaches college poetry and self-empowerment workshops for women. Ms. Hausman's work has been widely published in reviews and anthologies, as well as in her own collection of poetry, *A Born-Again Wife's First Lesbian Kiss and Other Poems* (Relief Press). She is past coordinator of poetry readings for the Bergen County Rape Crisis Center in New Jersey; her poems and short stories have been recorded and broadcast over Columbia University's Bank Street Radio in New York City. Her own spiritual quest has given her insight into the power of forgiveness and the blessing of letting go of the stronghold of anger. Her writing helps accomplish this.

**Paula Agranat Hurwitz** grew up in Massachusetts and lives in California. She has worked as a microbiology technician, stamp dealer, archivist and medical librarian. She is also a published composer, author and poet. An abuse survivor with multiple personality disorder, she has recently published two art therapy "coloring books" for abuse survivors and for multiples. In her spare time, she is a paraprofessional mental health counselor and does extensive research in the psychology of adult survivors of abuse and on the dissociative disorders. Paula is divorced and the mother of two grown sons. She has been in therapy for nine years dealing with inter- and intra-familial sexual abuse and the resulting emergence of multiple personality disorder. Her progress toward a healthier and more fulfilling life has been slow, but there is great improvement.

**Janit** is a writer, storyteller and facilitator of creative expression in the Pacific North West. She lives totally and fully in each moment with expectancy and integrity.

**Tessa Katz** was born in Cape Town , South Africa. She currently works as a Homeopath and a Family Physician in London, England. She is Jewish Lesbian Feminist, whose heart still lies with the struggle in South Africa, despite living in London at pres-

## Contributor Notes

ent. Her feminist politics were fostered by her work in rape crisis in Cape Town, and she has continued this commitment to a feminist way of working by running the Women's Clinic at the Royal London Homeopathic Hospital (a national health service hospital for complementary medicine). She has an identical twin sister and two older brothers.

**Nancy Lee**, a native of Yonkers, New York, is now a resident of Pittsburgh, Pennsylvania. She is grateful to Karen L. for supporting her through the darkest days, and to Craig for helping her to pick up the pieces and learn to smile.

**Frances Louis** is a pseudonym for a novelist and short story writer who has published a feminist satire. Her second novel was published in spring 1997. Although the piece, "Doors," was a difficult one to write, the writer gives thanks to the support of her husband and her therapist who continue to help her find a healing space. Because she maintains a relationship (however tentative) with her brother, the writer has decided to conceal her identity but looks forward to the day when she will be able to write about these incidents without feeling the conflicted desire both to tell the truth and protect those who contributed to the abuse.

**Diane McMahon**, born in North Vancouver, B.C., is currently studying art and working on her writing.

**Michelle** grew up in New York City. At present, she lives in Stamford, Connecticut. Since the birth of her two children, she has devoted her time to raising her children and her recovery from sexual abuse. Michelle is a published poet and has written several short stories. She is a licensed massage therapist and has a full time practice. A large percentage of her practice is devoted to teaching her clients to listen and trust their bodies.

# Contributor Notes

**Nancy** is an artist and writer, living and working in the Detroit area. As a child, Nancy won several awards for art and creative writing, and throughout high school and college continued to be awarded for academic and artistic excellence. She graduated cum laude from Wayne State University with a Bachelor of Fine Arts. Nancy used art, as she often does today, as a way of expressing and surviving the pain of incest during her childhood. Today, Nancy shows her paintings at galleries while participating in local and national competitions. Her studio is home-based, where her daughter and best critic is always present.

**NíAódagaín** is a lesbian writer and recently co-edited *All of Secrets Exposed: Southern Oregon Women Writing on Abuse and Molestation*. In putting pen to paper, she "breaks the silence." She encourages others to do the same so that, together, our voices, our stories, and ultimately our lives cannot be denied.

**Patten O'Brien** was born and raised in a small town in the Midwest. She is the youngest of three children of Catholic parents and the only girl. After graduating from Bryn Mawr College, she spent several years in Asia. She now lives in the United States and works in international education. She was first molested by a teenage neighbor boy when she was 3 years old. She was incested by her eldest brother off and on between the ages of 6 and 12. She was molested once more by a stranger at the age of 12. She has always remembered her incest and molestations. Her desire to create a family of her own has given her the clarity and determination to force her parents and brothers to face her abuse. She felt their incest had to be brought into the open before she could consider bringing children of her own into the family.

**M. Omura**. No biography.

## Contributor Notes

**Lynne Phoenix** lives in Takoma Park, Maryland, balancing motherhood, loverhood, and livelihood. When there is time, she loves to write and draw.

**Tzarina T. Prater** lives in New Jersey where she is pursuing a doctorate in literature at Rutgers University.

**Christine Anne Pratt** was born in Boston, Massachusetts, March 9th, 1950, and spent her childhood in a small, rural town near the ocean. After pursuing an interest in theater, she went back to school in her mid-twenties and received a B.A. from Goddard College with concentrations in creative writing and psychology, followed by an M.A. in counseling from Antioch New England. She lives and works in western Massachusetts.

**Ann Russek** has an M.F.A. in creative writing from the University of Alaska. She is a part-time faculty member at Muhlenberg College in Allentown in southeastern Pennsylvania. Her poetry has appeared in *The 1993 Anthology of New England Poets, the Cincinnati Poets' Collective, Verse, Chants*, and many other national and regional publications. This is her first poem dealing with the survival of incest.

**C.S.** No biography.

**Jeanne Savage** was brought up in a Manhattan suburb in the World War II era. She suffered incest and other abuse as a child. The victimization contributed to erratic performance in school and poor socialization skills. Carrying low esteem into adulthood, she "managed." She attended a small college in her forties and graduated as a registered nurse in 1983.

**Risa Shaw** celebrated her 40th birthday with a bonfire and sledding. A Jewish, lesbian, feminist who grew up in Kansas and Nebraska, she was raised with mixed messages to always speak out and never speak out.

# Contributor Notes

**Jennifer Corse Simon**, poet, artist, singer and witch is a stay-at-home mom with her new son, Griffin and her husband, rock musician and policy analyst, Russ Simon. They live in Albany, New York.

**Judy Stein**, born in the year 1995, a whole, healthy, dynamic woman!

**Catherine Swanson** is a divorced mother of two beautiful children ages 17 and 13. At 51, she has worked through the issues described in her poetry and is now working as a freelance writer, enjoying life, her family and the freedom that has come with age. She still writes poems on occasion, to satisfy her creative needs. Her poems have been published in the journals *Up Against the Wall, Peregrine,* and *Mother,* and in the book, *The Writer As An Artist.*

**Patti Tana** is a professor of English at Nassau Community College (SUNY) and the author of five books of poetry: *How Odd This Ritual of Harmony* (1981), *Ask The Dreamer Where Night Begins* (1986), *The River* (1990), *Wetlands* (1993), and *When the Light Falls Short of the Dream* (1998).

**Ruth Trevarrow** is an artist and arts organizer in Washington, DC. She came out about being a survivor of sexual abuse after getting sober in 1985. Before getting sober and dealing with the incest, she mostly drew in black and white. She has used art to heal, and to speak her mind. Her most recent works include a set of Gay American History Stamps, and the exhibition *Too Queer: Interrogating the Border Guards of Queer Identity.* She especially enjoys working on community projects with writers, performers, and other artists.

**Blanche Woodbury** has made poetry central to her life since the age of 15. She teaches creative writing and women's studies at a liberal arts college in central New York State.

# Resources

Resources are abundant, but they can be difficult for survivors to locate. It can take guts and time and money to access them. If you can pick up a phone, open your mouth, lay your hands on the books and/or access the Internet, you will find that the information is there.

Try the following: local rape crisis centers; women's studies programs and offices at colleges and universities; web sites; local libraries; and resource sections in other books. *The Courage to Heal*, by Ellen Bass and Laura Davis, has an extensive resource section at the back of the text that is well worth looking at.

Be tenacious and don't give up—find what you are looking for, even if you are not sure what it is.